Fusion Fashion

Gertrud Lehnert / Gabriele Mentges (eds.)

Fusion Fashion
Culture beyond Orientalism
and Occidentalism

Bibliographic Information published by the Deutsche Nationalbibliothek
The Deutsche Nationalbibliothek lists this publication in the Deutsche Nationalbibliografie;
detailed bibliographic data is available in the internet at http://dnb.d-nb.de.

Cover illustration: © Pravina Shukla

Typesetting: Daniel Devoucoux

Library of Congress Cataloging-in-Publication Data

Fusion fashion : culture beyond orientalism and occidentalism / Gertrud Lehnert/Gabriele Mentges (eds.).
  pages cm
  One contribution in French.
  Includes bibliographical references.
  Summary: „The focus of „Fusion Fashion" is on Orientalism as a sartorial practice, which has to be differentiated from the common knowledge of/on Orientalism by means of its organization, constitution and reception. The book offers historic as well as systematic perspectives. On the one hand, it compares orientalizing practices in fashion since the Tang period in China and European Renaissance. On the other hand, it highlights current tendencies of so called „orientalism", „self-orientalism", „occidentalism" in a globalized world. The book covers two time periods: Orientalized fashion practices from the 16th to the beginning of the 20th century, with an emphasis on European „Oriental" practices, and the period beginning in the 1990s up to the present day, with an emphasis on non-Western sartorial practices"— Provided by publisher.
  ISBN 978-3-631-60975-0 ISBN 978-3-653-03343-4 (e-book) 1. Fashion Asian influences. 2. Fashion Asia. 3. Fasion Europe. 4. Exoticism in fashion. 5. Orientalism. 6. Europe Civilization Oriental influences. I. Lehnert, Gertrud, editor of compilation. II. Mentges, Gaby, 1952- editor of compilation. III. Chen, Buyun. Toward a definition of „fashion" in Tang China (618-907 CE).
GT511.F87 2013
391 dc23

2013018781

ISBN 978-3-631-60975-0 (Print)
E-ISBN 978-3-653-03343-4 (E-Book)
DOI 10.3726/978-3-653-03343-4

© Peter Lang GmbH
Internationaler Verlag der Wissenschaften
Frankfurt am Main 2013
All rights reserved.
PL Academic Research is an Imprint of Peter Lang GmbH.

Peter Lang – Frankfurt am Main · Bern · Bruxelles · New York ·
Oxford · Warszawa · Wien

All parts of this publication are protected by copyright. Any
utilisation outside the strict limits of the copyright law, without
the permission of the publisher, is forbidden and liable to
prosecution. This applies in particular to reproductions,
translations, microfilming, and storage and processing in
electronic retrieval systems.

www.peterlang.de

Contents

Gertrud Lehnert / Gabriele Mentges: Fusion Fashion. Culture beyond Orientalism and Occidentalism   7

Buyun Chen: Toward a definition of „fashion" in Tang China (618-907 CE)   15

Gabriele Mentges: Drawing Borders: Perceptions of the Cultural Other in Renaissance Costume Books   27

Gertrud Lehnert: Orientalism in the 18th and 19th Century Fashion Magazines   49

Mona Abaza: The Motahajiba in Cairo, Inter-Arab Islamic chic, Adaptation, Hybridity and Globalization   71

Pravina Shukla: Fashion in the East: Dress in Modern India   89

Yuniya Kawamura: The Globalization of Japanese Lolita Fashion   105

Oly Firsching-Tovar: Reviving Kimono: Fashion as Memory at the Turn of the Twenty-First Century   117

Daniel Devoucoux: Bollywood, ou la réinvention de l'orientalisme et de l'occidentalisme dans le cinéma indien actuel   131

Summaries   151
Biographies   157
List of Illustrations   161

Fusion Fashion: Culture beyond Orientalism and Occidentalism

Gertrud Lehnert / Gabriele Mentges

Oriental goods and alterity

Fashion as a dynamic consists predominantly of change and the emergence of novelties. The Cabinet des Modes declares this in form of a motto on each title page: „L'ennui nacquit un jour de l'uniformité". In 1789, they compare English fashion to French fashion. English fashions never change – the French magazine declares! - because the English look for perfection: „pour varier, il faudroit mille essais, les essais ne peuvent pas avoir la perfection, et ils y renoncent". The French, in contrast, would be extremely bored by perfection, so their fashions change all the time ... [1] Fashion's purpose, besides the apparent economic one, is to offer new perceptions and to engender fantasies (an aesthetic and a psychological argument).

Within this conceptual frame, oriental elements served, since the crusades, as a driving force behind what was to become Western fashion. Oriental luxury goods could easily fill the need for alterity and social distinction. They were, from the very beginning, seen as luxurious because they were hard to obtain, expensive and rare. They were endowed with qualities like sensuality, fairytale fantasy, passion and civilization, as well as with the opposite: wildness, perversion and excess. The exotic was feared and desired at the same time and soon incarnated the fantastic otherness *par excellence*, the object of desire very distant from contemporary familiar life. And yet, quickly incorporated, it could rapidly become part of the familiar and thus be devoid of its menacing aspects.[2] However, the oriental textiles as carrier of new knowledge about technologies of production and fibres also meant a challenge to Western Europe. In the 16th century Europeans started to imitate and to copy the quality of the imported textiles and rapidly became serious competitors for their Eastern partners in the trade of luxury goods.[3] The ambivalence between admiration and competition ,and even fear, is deeply engrained in the Western adoption of the exotic. Against all probability, exotic objects have – more or less – kept these attributions until today, although the knowledge about them has increased: the knowledge about their material features, about the regions from which they

---

1 Cabinet 1789, 1. mars, p. 76.
2 In a political context, it could be used for specific purposes, as Ina McCabe (2008) has demonstrated.
3 Walter B. Denny: Oriental carpets and Textiles in Venice. In: Venice and the Islamic World 828-1797. The Metropolitan Museum of Art New York and London 2007, p. 174-191, p. 183.

come, about how they are produced (and later imitated), as well as about the ways the ideas they embody are constructed as images and clichés in order to serve different power politics. Nevertheless, their 'fantastic' image remains. From an individual psychological perspective one could call that process repression. We know (intellectually) how things work, but we don't want to realize it. And this is exactly why things can retain their power and become the agent of individual behaviour as well as of cultural processes. Sigmund Freud's linkage of psychoanalysis with culture as well as Carl Gustav Jung's theory of the archetypes laid some of the foundations for modern ethnopsychology discussing what Mario Erdheim calls the "social production of the unconscious"[4]. It has, however, as far as we know, not yet been applied to the analysis of Orientalism/exoticism with regard to dress and fashion.

Oriental sartorial practices and the West

We claim that the specific sartorial practices of Orientalism differ from other forms of Orientalism, therefore their analysis must be different. In our understanding, textile artefacts and fashion items count among the most essential objects of material culture. These artefacts reveal and visualize a specific cultural knowledge, including technologies. They serve not only as display for prestige and luxury, but their sheer materiality and contact with the body invite a specific sensual confrontation with otherness. In this book, we want to follow what Serge Gruzinski has once called "the track of sartorial artefacts"[5]. We argue that sartorial practices submerge fundamental premises of traditional conceptions of Orientalism equating - for example – the representation and the appropriation of oriental objects with hegemony, or conflating "distance" with otherness, proximity with the self. Further, we put forward the argument that the contact of "East and West" via fashion requires one to redefine boundaries between the other and the self, between strangeness and familiarity. And, coming back to the argument that the desire for alterity as well as for difference and distinction drives fashion, we also have to ask whether alterity is inevitably linked to hegemony and power.

This perspective may invite reconsideration of Edward Said's argument of "Orientalism" as a pure social construction because it does not refer to the empirical material conditions of Orientalism. If new postcolonial studies rightly require that the other be allowed to speak [6] we have to ask who are in fact the

---

4 Mario Erdheim: Die gesellschaftliche Produktion von Unbewußtheit. Eine Einführung in den ethnopsychologischen Prozeß, Frankfort 1982.
5 Serge Gruzinski: La pensée métisse. Paris 1999.$
6 Sebastian Conrad / Shalini Randeria: Geteilte Geschichten – Europa in einer postkolonialen Welt. In: Conrad/Randeria (Hg.): Jenseits des Eurozentrismus. Postkoloniale Perspektiven in den Geschichts- und Kulturwissenschaften, Frankfurt/Main 2001, p. 9-49, p. 12-13.

others in fashion, who the „Orientals" and who their European counterparts? Spivak's term "representation" aids us in mastering the ambivalence in fashion practices and discourses: on one hand representation means performance, on the other it inherently claims to replace the other.[7] In fashion, both dualistic practices are perfectly linked because with the body they involve all senses of the actors. Thus, it is another way to live and to experience difference and the other, with different meanings and goals depending on each particular historical constellation. This connection could help to explain why in times when, during the 18th century, the Turks of the Ottoman empire were attacking Western European powers, Europeans were so fond of Turkish dress and fabrics.

At least, we should identify and create a clear distinction between the different historical actors and their practices. In other words, what does oriental fashion mean to the European bourgeois lady wearing a Turkish style head scarf or coat? What effects did Poiret's presentation of oriental haute couture have during his visit to the United States in the beginning of the 20th century for Orientalism as discourse and practice? Does the incorporation of oriental design into European fashion help to forge European identity via dress?

The Book

Older studies deal mostly with the contrast between Orientalism and Western fashion cultures (e.g, Richard Martin and Harold Koda 1994; Steele/ Major 1999). More recent studies on Orientalism focus either on special cultures or societies (Tarlo 2010), on particular historical periods (McCabe 2008) or on theoretical questions (race and Orientalism, e.g. Kondo 1997). Fashion is often not the main topic, but only a means to illustrate processes of orientalization (Berg 2005; Berg 2008, Riello 2009 a, Riello 2009 b).

$In contrast, the focus of this book is only in part the history of Orientalism. Its main objective is to present tendencies which can be labeled "entangled fashion" in analogy to the concept of "entangled fashion", or "fusion fashion". Fashion can no longer be regarded as a modern phenomenon only to be found in the West. Fashion theory has to reconsider the distribution of signs and values within the globalized consumer culture and the politics of their exchange. We have to avoid substituting one paradigm for another as, for example, turning the Euro-centric perspective into the paradigm of an Asian-Euro-centric view.

---

7 For Gayatri Spivak: Can the subalternal speak. in: Cary Nelson/Lawrence Grossberg (ed.)_ Marxisme and the interpretation of culture. London 1988, p.271- 313, p.275 quote after Conrad/Randieria (ed.), op.cit., p. 23. Spivak's definition of representation: "Two senses of representation are run together: representation as "speaking for", as in politics, and representation as "re-presentation, as in art or philosophy.

The history of fashion has begun to be re-written in a global perspective.[8] We hope to contribute to that new concept of fashion beyond the traditional Western concept.

Orientalism as an important part of Euro-centric perspectives on culture and history implicitly suggests that global history is organized around *Western* history. On the other hand it presupposes the Western modernization process to be a generalized or generalizable schema.[9]

With the selected examples of orientalizing sartorial practices, we hope to contribute to the re-writing of the history of *material* culture in another than the "orientalised and Euro-centered" perspectives and to discover the different voices of a multiple other: we suggest thinking of it in terms of "entangled history".[10] How does fashion as a *concept* work, and how does it relate to "Orientalism"? For this reason we think it necessary to widen and deepen the history of fashion by including the role of fashion magazines, fashion photography, movies and so on. It is also necessary to systematically analyze the signification of subcultures for the fashion system and to reconsider the essential part of global trade in a historical perspective.

The focus of "Fusion Fashion" is therefore on Orientalism as a sartorial practice, which has to be differentiated from the common concepts of Orientalism in terms of organization, constitution and reception. The book offers historic as well as systematic perspectives. On the one hand, it compares the beginnings of orientalizing practices in fashion since the Renaissance and discusses the contribution of early fashion magazines to the discourse of Orientalism. On the other hand, it highlights current tendencies of so called "Orientalism", "self-Orientalism", "Occidentalism" in a globalized world. The book covers two time periods: Orientalized fashion practices from the 16th to the beginning of the 20th century, with an emphasis on European „oriental" practices, and the period beginning in the 1990s up to the present day, with an emphasis on non-Western sartorial practices.

---

[8] See, among others: Marie Leshkowich, Sandra Niessen, Carla Jones: Re-Orienting Fashion: The Globalization of Asian Dress. Oxford: Berg 2003, Giorgio Riello, Peter McNeill (eds.): The Fashion History Reader. Global Perspectives, London, New York 2010; Kristin Knox: Culture to Catwalk. How World Cultures influence Fashion, London 2011; Jan Brand, José Teunissen (eds.): Global Fashion - Local Tradition. On the Globalization of Fashion, Arnhem: Terra 2005; Gertrud Lehnert: Karneval der Stile / Über "Global Fashion - Local Tradition. On the Globalization of Fashion" in: Texte zur Kunst 78, Juni 2010, 162-165.

[9] For a global history see Jürgen Osterhammel: Die Entzauberung Asiens. Europa und die asiatischen Reiche im 18. Jahrhundert, München 2010 (including a critical epilogue on Eurocentric Orientalism); Jürgen Osterhammel: Die Verwandlung der Welt. Eine Geschichte des 19. Jahrhunderts, München 2011.

[10] For a good definition of entangled history see Conrad, Sebastian/Randeria, Shalini (ed.): Jenseits des Eurozentrismus. Postkoloniale Perspektiven in den Geschichts- und Kulturwissenschaften, Frankfurt/Main, 2001, p.17

Theoretical premises

The following assumptions outline the objectives of this book:

Fashion is used as a means for cultural inclusion and exclusion. Western fashion has long claimed an aesthetic, technical as well as moral/ethical superiority over the non-western sartorial otherness.

European fashion, however, has always adopted 'oriental' practices yet in different ways and with different goals. Moreover, the development of European fashion is substantially due to the cultural transfer of techniques, materials, tastes and aesthetics.

Thus, fashion contributes to specific constructions of Orientalism through the sensual and ambivalent character of its materiality and the ambiguity of consumption practices.

A characteristic feature of Orientalism as a sartorial practice is to be found in the close link between fashion, politics and economy. These spheres have to be understood as programmatic spaces of representation and thus facilitate strategies of cultural identity formation.

On the other hand, Western fashion has become very influential in non-Western societies in the course of colonialism and globalization. The process of appropriation of Western fashion can be described with Homi K. Bhabha's concept of „mimicry" or, as Michael Taussig proclaims, as „a mimetic exchange with the world"[11] and hence as an active and sensual incorporation of the Other.

Yet, current processes of 'Re-Orientalizing the Orient' and the 'Return of the Local' cannot be reduced to a mere response to the hegemony of Western fashion. Beyond „re-ethnicization" or „folklorization", they are new cultural strategies within the post-colonial space, which point to the complex positioning of the cultural and social self within the global fashion system. But can Bhabha's concept of "third space" be usefully employed in the analysis of fashion as a global phenomenon?

Terminology

"Fusion Culture", in our understanding, designates multiple ways of transnational contacts and exchange, narrations, of making selections from foreign cultures, of fragmenting, of incorporating - or rejecting - the "other", of

---

11 Homi Bhabha: The Location of Culture, London, New York 1993 ; Michael Taussig: Mimesis and Alterity: A particular history of the senses, New York, London: Routledge 1993.

merging and thus changing certain aspects of different cultures – an open process without ever coming to an end. Fusion Culture is comparable to Homi Bhabha's concept of "third space", but "fusion culture" seemed more appropriate with regard to fashion. We do, however, continue to use the term "oriental" as a working term in a double sense as:

1. related to the artefacts originating in the region the Enlightenment defined as "Orient": Asian and Arabian cultures and Persia: more or less everything "east of Europe", as says the Encyclopédie. Oriental material culture was exported to the West and integrated into and incorporated in European consumption practices.

2. Orientalism is employed as a discursive element as introduced by Edward Said, meaning the construction of oriental otherness by colonial practices and knowledge. However, our aim is to question Said's concepts as well as the theoretical amendments and corrections which were added later by post-colonial studies and the new consumption studies.

The various chapters discuss traditional concepts of Orientalism in different historical periods and explore their impact on the European societies as well as on fashion in general within a global framework. They provide examples of the reinforcement of European identity by the means of moral exclusion of the other's body and taste and by the means of distance between centre and periphery in Renaissance costume books (Mentges), present fashion magazines as a place to imagine and to represent the variety of European selves and European differences (Lehnert). Contemporary phenomena are discussed: the global trend and national model of Japanese Lolita (Kawamura) and the revival of old dress traditions like the kimonos in Japan (Tovar). Other articles show the impact of consumer culture on Islamic fashion in Egypt (Abaza) or the role and influence of Bollywood movies on the creation of fusion fashion in India and at the same time reinforcement of an Indian identity (Devoucoux). Finally, Buyun Shen argues that fashion is no modern Western phenomenon, but that even in ancient cultures (like in Chinese Tang Dynasty – 7th to 10th century a. C.) one can find phenomena very closely related to the modern concept of fashion as self-fashioning. Thus she refutes the traditional conviction that Chinese traditional dress was mainly composed of ritual garments. For modern times, the contribution of Shukla conveys how traditional sartorial dress practices in India are based on the narrow exchange between producer, trade and consumer respecting changes of taste and new influences as well.

The following book is partly based on the conference " Fusion Fashion. Beyond Orientalism and Occidentalism at the University of Potsdam from November 5-7 2009,, with financial support of the Volkswagen Stiftung to whom we express our gratitude for their generous grant.

Bibliography

Benjamin, Roger (2003), Orientalist Aesthetics: Art, Colonialism and French North Africa (Berkeley and Los Angeles, California U.P.)
Baghdiantz McCabe, Ina: Orientalism in Early Modern France. Eurasian Trade, Exoticism, and the Ancien Régime. Oxford: Berg 2008
Berg, Maxime: Luxury and Pleasure in Eighteenth-Century Britain. Oxford: Oxford University Press 2005
Berg, Maxine / Eger, Elizabeth (Hg.): Luxury in the Eighteenth-Century: Debates, Desires and Delectable Goods. Basingstoke, u.a.: Palgrave 2008
Bhabha, Homi: The Location of Culture, London, New York, Routledge, 1993
Brewer, John / Porter, R. (Hg.): Consumption and the World of Goods. New York: Routledge 1993
Brydon, A. / Niessen, S.: Consuming Fashion: Adorning the Transnational Body. Oxford: Berg 1998
Cabinet des modes, ou les modes nouvelles, starting nov. 1785
Conrad, Sebastian/Randeria, Shalini (ed.): Jenseits des Eurozentrismus. Postkoloniale Perspektiven in den Geschichts- und Kulturwissenschaften, Frankfurt/Main 2001: Campus
Denny, Walter B.: Oriental carpets and Textiles in Venice. Venice and the Islamic World 828-1797. The Metropolitan Museum of Art New York /London 2007, p- 174-191
Erdheim, Mario: Die gesellschaftliche Produktion von Unbewußtheit. Eine Einführung in den ethnopsychologischen Prozeß, Frankfurt: Suhrkamp 1982
Fashion Theory. The Journal of Dress, Body and Culture, Vol. 7, Issues 4 and 4, ed. Nirmal Puwar, Nandi Bhatia, 2003
Global Fashion - Local Tradition. On the Globalization of Fashion, ed. Jan Brand, José Teunissen, Arnhem: Terra 2005, 2. Aufl 2006
Gruzinski, Serge: La pensée métisse. Paris 1999
Hackforth-Jones, Jos, / Roberts, Mary (2004) (eds), Edges of Empire: Orientalism and Visual Culture (Oxford, Blackwell)
Kawamura, Yuniya: The Japanese Revolution in Paris Fashion, Oxford, New York 2004
Kawamura, Yuniya (2005): Fashion-ology, An Introduction to Fashion Studies, Oxford, New York: Berg
Koda, Harold / Richard Martin: Orientalism. Visions of the East in Western Dress, New York: The Metropolitan Museum of Art 1994
Kondo, Dorinne (1997), About Face: performing race in Fashion and Theatre (London, Routledge)
Lehnert, Gertrud: Mode als Medium des Kulturtransfers im 18. Jahrhundert, in: Höfe — Salons — Akademien. Kulturtransfer und Gender im Europa der Frühen Neuzeit, hg. Margarete Zimmermann, Gesa Stedmann, Hildesheim (Olms Verlag) 2007, 309-340

Lehnert, Gertrud: Des "robes à la turque" et autres orientalismes à la mode, in : Anja Bandau/Marcel Dorigny/Rebekka von Mallinckrodt (ed.). Les mondes coloniaux à Paris au XVIIIe siècle. Circulation et enchevêtrement des savoirs, Paris: Karthala 2010, 183-200

Lehnert, Gertrud: Karneval der Stile / Über "Global Fashion - Local Tradition. On the Globalization of Fashion" in: Texte zur Kunst 78, Juni 2010, 162-165

Marie Leshkowich, Sandra Niessen, Carla Jones: Re-Orienting Fashion: The Globalization of Asian Dress. Oxford: Berg 2003

Low, Gail Ching-Liang (1996), White Skins/Black Masks: Representation and Colonialism (London, Routledge)

McCabe, Ina Baghdiantz: Orientalism in Early Modern France. Eurasian Trade, Exoticism, and the Ancien Régime, Oxford, NY: Berg 2008

Mentges, Gabriele: Kulturanthropologie des Textilen, Berlin/Dortmund 2005.

Mentges, Gabriele: Massgeschneiderte Identität. In: Die Welt als Laufsteg. Mode und Identität. Zeitschrift für Kulturaustausch. 52. Jg. 4/2002, p.52-55

Mentges, Gabriele: Der Kopftuchstreit. In: Hinz, Renate/Walthes, Renate (Hg.): Verschiedenheit als Diskurs. Tübingen 2011, p. 215-224

Niessen, S. / Leshkowich, A. M. / Jones, C. 2003: Re-Orienting Fashion: The Globalization of Asian Dress

Riello, Giorgio (ed.): The Spinning World: A Global History of Cotton Textiles, 1200-1850, Oxford: Oxford University Press, 2009 a (with Prasannan Parthasarathi)

Riello, Giorgio (ed.), How India Clothed the World: The World of South Asian Textiles, 1500-1850; Leiden: Brill, 2009 b (with Tirthankar Roy)

Riello, Giorgio / McNeil, Peter (eds.) (2010): The Fashion History Reader. Global Perspectives, London; New York: Routledge

Said, Edward: Orientalism (1994), New York, Vintage Books

Scarce, Jennifer (1987), Women's Costume of the Near and Middle East (London, Unwin Hyman)

Steele, Valerie / Major, John S.: China Chic: East Meets West. New Haven: Yale UP, 1999

Tarlo, Emma: Visibly Muslim. Fashion, Politics, Faith: Bodies of Faith, London: A&C Black 2010

Taussig, Michael: Mimesis and Alterity: A particular history of the senses, New York, London: Routledge 1993

Venice and the Islamic World 828-1797. (2007) The Metropolitan Museum of Art (ed.), New York /London: Yale University Press.

Wollen, Peter (1987) 'Fashion/Orientalism/The Body'New Formations 1, Spring

Toward a definition of "fashion" in Tang China (618-907 CE)

BuYun Chen

In the late eighth century, a woman of the Tang court would have emerged from her boudoir in a short, fitted brocade jacket paired with a high-waisted, striped A-line skirt. Just a few decades later, the palace women of the Tang emperor Xianzong's court (805-820) abandoned the slim silhouettes of their predecessors, opting for broad sleeves and billowy skirts sewn from silk-netted gauze. Lean figures were now rendered obsolete by the voluptuous bodies of the new regime of fashion. Describing the old palace maid as a hopelessly dated figure, the mid-Tang poet Bai Juyi (772-846) lamented: "Her slippers like pointed peaks, her gown tight-fitting/With dark pigment she paints slender, long brows/If the people outside were to see her, they would even laugh/For her out-of-date dress belongs to the former Tianbao [742-756] era."[1] The maid's attire assumes a metonymic role for her expired body, highlighting the power of dress in situating the body "in time" or in this case, "out of time." Dramatic shifts in the modes of dress from the eighth to ninth centuries led to an experience of being "in time" (rushi) or "timely" (shishi) that was bound to the fashionable body. And it is in this language of bodies, time, and changing styles that one can hear the murmurs of a nascent fashion system.

4Discussions of dress in pre-twentieth century China have long reduced dress to a ritualistic, performative function – as "costume" – that is immune to the rules of fashion-as-change. In his monumental study of the "structures of everyday life," Fernand Braudel argued that the history of costume "touches on every issue – raw materials, production processes, manufacturing costs, cultural stability, fashion and social hierarchy."[2] For Braudel, fashion was a phenomenon unique to the West. China, however, belonged to the timeless rest-of-the-world in which dress "scarcely changed in the course of centuries."[3] The myth of a static Chinese costume was part and parcel of a more pervasive critique of an inert Chinese society immobilized by tradition, a view that was also embraced by modern Chinese intellectuals. In a 1943 article, the celebrated writer Eileen Chang anticipated Braudel when she wrote, "generation after generation of women wore the same sorts of clothes without feeling in the least

---

1 Bai Juyi, "The White-haired Maid of Shangyang Palace," in Quan Tangshi [Complete Tang Poems], vol. 13 (Shanghai: Zhonghua shuju, 1960), 4692.
2 Fernand Braudel, Civilization and Capitalism, 15th- 18th Centuries, Vol. 1: The Structures of Everyday Life, trans. Sian Reynolds (London: Collins, 1981), 311.
3 Ibid, 312.

perturbed."[4] The failure of the Chinese to change their clothing was evidence of the country's greater inability to modernize like Europe. Just as "fashion" was equated with industrial West, "costume" was relegated to the non-modern East.

Recent scholars have attempted to reclaim fashion from the West, redefining it as a technique of the self that emerged in different places at different times.[5] In a similar shift, this chapter construes fashion broadly as a system of social practices that is governed by material conditions. In the larger work on which this chapter is based, I argue that fashion's rise in the mid-Tang dynasty signaled a process in which competition for status and self-identification among the elites gradually broke away from the imperial court and its system of official ranks, catalyzing a desire for novelty that transformed the dressed body into a stage for status display. The decline of the empire, beginning in the latter half of the eighth century, forced elite members of society to seek new avenues for exhibiting power and wealth. Sartorial savvy became one arena for competition between the old aristocracy and new military or merchant elite. The emergence of fashion during the Tang dynasty mirrored socioeconomic changes associated with the rise of early modern European fashion, such as an increase in the variety of commercial goods, specifically luxury goods, and the increased speed with which they changed. Nowhere was this more evident than in the expansion of the silk economy during the latter half of the dynasty, enabled by the breakdown of both the imperial workshops and the controlled market system.

Social competition and economic growth spurred vestimentary change, but underpinning the whole was a desire to dress a la mode. And over the course of the dynasty, the market expanded to incorporate new silhouettes, patterns, and fabrics, undermining the symbolic order of clothing and satisfying the impulse for fashion.

The Dress Code

In China as in Europe, the rise of fashion was predicated on transformations in the concept and construction of self. In Tang China, this shift found its clearest expression in the symbolic order of appearances in which fashion-as-social gradually supplanted fashion-as-material as the primary mode of sartorial behavior. As suggested by Ann Rosalind Jones and Peter Stallybrass in the context of Renaissance Europe, fashion-as-material implied a notion of clothing

---

4 Zhang Ailing [Eileen Chang], "A Chronicle of Changing Clothes," trans. Andrew F. Jones, positions: east asia cultures critique 11, 2 (Fall 2003), 429. First published in the Chinese journal Gujin in December 1943.

5 Arguing for a more inclusive definition of fashion, Jennifer Craik defines it as a system that fixes "the denotation of acceptable codes and conventions" and that "sets limits to clothing behaviour, prescribes acceptable – and proscribes unacceptable – modes of clothing the body, and constantly revises the rules of the fashion game." Jennifer Craik, The Face of Fashion: Cultural Studies in Fashion (New York: Routledge, 1994), 5.

as constitutive of personal identities that had no a priori existence.[6] Anything but superficial, clothes made the subject via "deep making," inscribing individual bodies with a specific set of relations and meanings. The livery servant, for example, was bound to his inner core to his master by wearing clothing bestowed by the latter. Fashion-as-social, by contrast, required a conception of clothing as a marker of an already-defined individual self that was capable of exercising personal choice. Within this context, clothing enabled a constant refashioning of the self through the subversion of sumptuary regulations. Throughout the Tang dynasty, the tension between fashion-as-material and fashion-as-social was articulated by the official prescriptions and proscriptions of court, ritual and everyday dress.

The "Treatise on Carriages and Dress," compiled by the official editors of the dynastic annals, serves as the official narrative of the clothing code, providing the basic lexicon for studies on a dynasty's dress. There exist two versions of the treatise for the Tang dynasty. The first belongs to the official chronicle, *Book of Tang*, originally completed in 945. In 1160, the dynastic history was revised and expanded as the *New Book of Tang*.[7] As both ritualized text and sumptuary legislation, the "Treatise on Carriages and Dress" belongs to the realm of "symbolic legislation" in which the existence of a body of laws is more significant than its actual enforcement.[8] The prescriptions of dress compiled in the treatise articulated an ideal of "stable status display" and a desire for the ordering of appearances, underscoring dress as an instrument of governance.

The concern with "stable status display" in the treatise developed from classical ritual texts such as the *Rites of Zhou*. Edited during the first few centuries of the Han dynasty, the *Rites of Zhou* shares with all subsequent sumptuary regulations an assumption that the categories of rulers and subjects are absolute. Objects are then assigned to these immutable categories. In the Tang "Treatise on Carriages and Dress," the categories are listed as follows: emperor, crown prince, officials (further divided according to rank), empress, crown princess, and court women. The treatise further identifies court (chaofu), official (gongfu), ritual (jifu/mianfu), and everyday (changfu) as the four primary genres of dress and adornment.[9] Within each generic division, the

---

6 Ann Rosalind Jones and Peter Stallybrass, Renaissance Clothing and the Materials of Memory (Cambridge: Cambridge University Press, 2000).

7 In order to accommodate the variations in the two versions of the Treatise on Carriages and Dress, selections from both the Book of Tang and New Book of Tang will be used to reconstruct an account of Tang women's dress.

8 See Susan Vincent, Dressing the Elite: Clothes in Early Modern England (New York: Berg, 2003), 143. Vincent's discussion of symbolic legislation derives from Alan Hunt's study on the relationship between sumptuary law and politics of governance. Alan Hunt, Governance of the Consuming Passions (New York: St. Martin's Press, 1996).

9 The treatises include lengthy descriptions of court and ritual dress, relegating little space to the genre of everyday dress.

treatise outlines the extensive inventory of articles to be worn according to rank, occasion, and season.[10]

Although the treatises regulate the attire of both male and female subjects of the court, the difficulties regarding womens' attire are particularly pertinent to the rise of the Tang fashion system. Women's ritual and everyday dress was expected to adhere to their husband's and son's standing in the system of "nine grades," which ranked civil and military officials serving the court. The dresscode restricted the availability of certain fabrics, trimmings, and the lengths of robes. The staples of the women's wardrobe included a skirt, blouse, jacket, and shawl, but the cuts, patterns, and accompanying adornments fluctuated according to period and region. The *New Book of Tang* provides the following set of rules governing women's dress:

> A woman's dress follows the ranking of her husband and son. Kin ranking closest to those in the fifth grade and above, including mothers and wives dress in purple robes, waist belts and sleeve bands of embroidered silk. Mothers and wives of those in the ninth grade and above wear cinnabar-colored robes. The officials outside of the nine grades and the commoners do not dress in silk damask, silk gauze, crepe silk, nor do they wear green, yellow, red, white, or black woven boots or slippers.[11]

On the surface, this account of everyday dress regulations suggests an absence of fashion. Sumptuary laws upheld social order by circumscribing the range of luxury and non-luxury goods made available to subjects depending on rank. The robes, accessories, and types of silk textiles allowed by the Tang dress code served to maintain visible distinctions, thereby reinforcing the fashion-as-material mode. This dress code, however, was repeatedly challenged inside and outside the gates of the palace. New trends, popularized through trade and a nascent market, regularly trickled into the wardrobe of the court propelling fashion-as-social forward.

Dressing Up Exotic

In the early Tang, a flirtation with western lifestyle and dress, specifically Central Asian and Sassanian styles, hinted at a budding desire to play the fashion game. The demand for foreign things in the late seventh and eighth

---

10 Although fashion historians of Europe have tended to consider special occasion attire such as court, official, and ritual clothing outside of the framework of fashion, these categories of dress will be treated as part of the Tang fashion system for the sheer reason that standardized court, official, and ritual clothing fluctuated according to larger trends circulating outside of the court. Women's court and official dress incorporated popular items of clothing. The banbi, a short-sleeved jacket, is a foremost example of an item of popular casual dress incorporated into the official ensemble of court women during the early Tang dynasty.

11 Ou Yangxiu, ed., "Treatise on Carriages and Dress," in Xin Tangshu [New Book of Tang], vol. 2 (Shanghai: Zhonghua shuju, 2006), 530.

centuries revealed an early impulse for fashion that was no longer bound to the social hierarchy and political order, challenging the officials' expressed desire to maintain rank by appearance. This exoticism, which communicated both an appetite for novelty and the potential of dress to re-make bodies, laid the foundation upon which the Tang fashion system would later flourish.

Trends imported from the west transformed and expanded the Tang vocabulary of dress. Trade facilitated the movement of new technologies and peoples into the empire, which led to fresh possibilities of dressing.[12] The establishment of the Silk Roads in the Han dynasty (206 BCE – 220 CE) secured the safe passage of ideas, goods, and technologies across political, cultural and geographic boundaries for several centuries. In the Tang dynasty, the route extended from the capital city, Chang'an, and skirted across Central Asia terminating in Antioch on the Mediterranean.[13] Tang expansion into the northwest, the establishment of peaceful trade, and political turmoil in the northwest and Central Asia displaced populations of merchants and craftsmen.[14] Prosperity in trade encouraged these migrants to relocate to the capital and the northwestern areas along the Silk Road. This environment enabled the exchange of ideas and skills, exhibited in the adoption and invention of new motifs and weaves by Tang artisans.[15]

Trade also filtered in new silhouettes. Characterized by tight sleeves, double lapels, and veiled hats, these new trends were classified as *hu* to mark their foreign origins.[16] Trapped in the anti-foreign sensitivities prevalent after the An

---

12 See Shen Congwen, Zhongguo gudai fushi yanjiu [Research on Classical Chinese Dress] (Hong Kong: Shangwu yinshu guan, 1992). For a thorough discussion of the influence of hu culture during the Tang dynasty, see Xiang Da, Tangdai Chang'an yu Xiyu wenming [The Civilizations of Tang Chang'an and the Western Region] (Beijing: Xinhua shudian, 1957).

13 Shelagh Vainker, Chinese Silk: A Cultural History (New Jersey: Rutgers University Press, 2004), 59.

14 See Morris Rossabi, "The Silk Trade in China and Central Asia," in When Silk Was Gold, ed. James CY Watt (New York: Metropolitan Museum of Art, 1997). Also, Rossabi, "Behind the Silk Screen: Movements of Weavers in Asia, Seventh to Fourteenth Centuries." Orientations, Vol. 29, No. 3 (March 1998), 84-89.

15 Sogdians, in particular, played a crucial role in the transmission of textile designs and technology. The Sogdians inhabited the areas of Bukhara, Samarkand, and Ferghana. During the fifth to eighth centuries, Turfan (in modern Xinjiang province) was home to the Sogdians, one of the two main immigrant groups. Han Chinese migrants from the Tang formed the other sizeable population in Turfan. As merchants, the Sogdians introduced Central Asian wool tapestries and indigo-dyed cotton murals as trade goods and inspired the integration of new textile designs with existing weave patterns. Sogdian artisans inhabiting strategic locations, particularly Turfan, collaborated with local and Tang-migrant artisans. See Angela Sheng, "Textile Finds Along the Silk Road," in The Glory of the Silk Road: Art from Ancient China, ed. Li Jian (Dayton: Dayton Art Institute, 2003) and Denis Sinor, ed., The Cambridge History of Early Inner Asia, (New York: Cambridge University Press, 1990).

16 Hu was used to as a general term refer to non-Chinese peoples settled to the north and west of the empire. See James C.Y. Watt, ed., Dawn of a Golden Age, 200 – 750 AD, (New

Lushan Rebellion of 755, during which a Sogdian-Turkic general nearly toppled the dynasty, the discussion of foreign trends provided by the *Book of Tang* and *New Book of Tang* tend to describe the popularity of *hu* style as an omen of the empire's demise. The narrative of the *hu* obsession, despite its discriminating tone, attests to the enduring popularity of *hu* fashion. Popular fetishization of *hu* extended to music, dance, sports, and food. Clothing was one feature of the *hu* lifestyle that was consumed by the early- to mid-Tang court. Notable additions to Tang fashion included the *weimao*, a wide brimmed hat commonly paired with a thin veil of gauze, and the *hufu*, a caftan-like robe worn by men and women. The *New Book of Tang* dates the introduction of the *weimao* to the early reign of emperor Gaozong (r. 650-683):

> At the beginning [of the Tang], women donned the mili17 to conceal their bodies. During the Yonghui era [650-655], they started to wear the weimao, the veil of which extended only to the neck. 18

The treatise goes on to chart the evolution of *hu* style at court:

> During the reign of Empress Wu [690-705], the weimao was exceptionally popular. After Zhongzhong [705-710], no one wore the mili again. The palace women and the emperor's attendants, all wore hu hats to ride horses and all within the empire imitated this. Then the women exposed their hair, tied in topknots, to go horse riding and the weimao was abandoned. They dressed in men's robes and boots, similar to the dress of the Xi and Khitans.[19]

The popularity of equestrianism in the early Tang formed the foundation for the rise of *hu* fashion in the court. The emperor's horse-riding attendants first popularized the *weimao*, *hufu*, and related changes in hairstyles and makeup. So pervasive was this pursuit of exoticism that from the seventh through eighth century, depictions of female musicians and attendants on horseback in tomb art are often attired in *hu* fashions to reflect the styles at the court. Once adopted by the women in the palace, the equestrian fashions of the *hu* spread beyond the court:

> At the beginning of the Kaiyuan period [713 – 741], the emperor's female horse-riding attendants all wore hu hats, with beautifully made up faces that were exposed. They did not conceal their faces again. The elites and commoners, as a result of this, again imitated the palace attendants. The institution of the weimao was never used while on the road. After a short while, the women started to expose their hair, which was tied in topknots, when they rode horses, and there were also those who dressed in men's robes, boots, and shirts. The aristocrats and the common women, the

---

York: Metropolitan Museum of Art, 2004). For brief summaries of different hu fashion, see Huang Zhengjian, Tangdai yi shi zhu xing yanjiu [Research on Everyday Life in the Tang Dynasty] (Beijing: Shou du shifan daxue chubanshe, 1998), 88-92.
17 Full-length veil worn to conceal the entire body.
18 Ou, ed., "Treatise on Carriages and Dress" [New Book of Tang], 531.
19 Ibid.

women inside and outside of the palace all partook in these styles without any distinction.20

The forces guiding fashionable dress here are identified as the court in general and women in particular.[21] As historian Huang Zhengjian has argued, the court was instrumental in popularizing new styles of adornment, like the *weimao*.[22] In the early Tang, this impulse to imitate the court alludes to the existence of an audience attuned to changes in dress. For clothing to function as a viable tool of "self-fashioning," such an audience was necessary. In order to be validated, one had to be observed. Competition over sartorial savvy depended on the participation of this audience as both knowledgeable spectators and copycats. Commoners, according to the official chronicles, also participated in the wearing of the *weimao* and dressing in men's riding garb. The courting of *hu* garments, across social hierarchies, suggested the collapse of the associations of fashionable dress with the bodies of Tang elite. The implication of this discourse is that fashion is a diffusion of an impulse to self-fashion.

Consumption of foreign things subsided slightly in the wake of the rebellion of 755, but remained present through the following centuries. The early Tang exoticism was still seen in the cuts and contours of late eighth century brocade robes that prominently featured variations on Central Asian motifs. The court, however, did not recover. The rebellion had crippled the empire politically and economically, resulting in the trafficking of people and wealth out of the capital and into the provinces. This restructuring of the political and commercial landscape weakened the aristocrats, who relied on stable, centralized imperial power to maintain their position in the social and fashion hierarchy.

Material Girls

By the ninth century, the declining court was displaced by the expanding silk industry as the motor of fashion. Transformations in the silk industry during the latter half of the Tang further drove fashion by supplying the fabrics for revising the rules of the fashion game to a wider sector of society. In particular, luxury silk production of the late eighth and nine centuries accommodated the self-

---

20 Liu Xu, ed., "Treatise on Carriages and Dress," in Jiu Tangshu [Book of Tang], vol. 6 (Shanghai: Zhonghua shuju, 1995), 1957.

21 Tang scholar Huang Zhengjian has argued that the main motive force of fashion were the court and aristocrats, citing Princess Anle's white-feathered skirt (毛裙) as an example. (Huang, 103) As attendants to the emperor, palace women had access to superior silks and weavers. The largest workshop producing silk within the palace was the department of seven hundred women who made brocade and embroidery for the palace ladies. [Shelagh Vainker, Chinese Silk: A Cultural History, 76-77.]

22 Huang Zhengjian, Tangdai yi shi zhu xing yanjiu, 103-4.

fashioning impulse of a new group of elites, composed of military officials and rich merchants.²³

Imperial and non-imperial production of silk reached an unprecedented height during the Tang dynasty. The development of new weaving devices, particularly looms capable of automatic repeats, and dyeing materials allowed for the production of novel silk textiles. Advances in silk weaving, however, were subject to sumptuary legislation. From the early decades of the dynasty, the state responded by enacting a series of unsuccessful attempts to curb luxury silk production. Edicts ordering the burning of looms, as well as frequent bans on the production and circulation of coveted silks, call attention to the conspicuous role of silk in the fashion system. The Tang dress code also aimed to limit access to silks, but was undermined by the transgressions of elite and non-elite women:

> When not in court, their manners [women of high ranking] are extravagant and excessive, and they do not conform to regulations and dress in damasks, silk gauzes, jin silk24, and embroidered silks according to their likes and tastes. Extending from court and reaching the commoners, [the women] all compete to imitate [the extravagant trends], and so, the aristocrats and the common people lack distinction.25

Here the voices of fashion-as-social can be detected. Women, embroiled in the politics of competition and imitation, subverted the regulations in order to dress in fine fabrics "according to their likes and tastes." This equation of extravagant dress with the wearing of damask, jin, and embroidered silks highlights the significant role of silk in the display of status.²⁶ For the Tang aristocracy, the wearing of sensuous silks was central to the articulation of status and power. Increased silk production during the Tang dynasty made this luxury item available outside the court, thereby loosening the aristocrats' grip on sensuous silks. The rise of weaving households, distributed across the three dominant regions of silk production following the dissolution of the imperial workshop during the latter half of the dynasty, was a leading factor in the

---

23 See Denis Twitchett, "The Composition of the T'ang Ruling Class," in Perspectives on the Tang, ed. Arthur Wright and Denis Twitchett (New Haven: Yale University Press, 1973). Also, Patricia B. Ebrey, The Aristocratic Families of Early Imperial China: A Case Study of the Po-ling Ts'ui Family (Cambridge: Cambridge University Press, 1978).

24 Jin (錦) refers to a general class of compound weaves similar to samite (weft-faced compound textile), however, there is no equivalent English term.

25 Liu, ed., "Treatise on Carriages and Dress" [Book of Tang], 1957.

26 In her survey on elite dress in early modern England, Susan Vincent has argued that clothing was fundamental to an individual's experience and creation of self. Echoing Jones and Stallybrass' concept of "deep making," Vincent defines dress as the medium through which the individual self took shape. This form of cultural production was a prerogative of the elite and apparel occupied a central position in the realization of power, wealth, and status. Susan Vincent, Dressing the Elite: Clothes in Early Modern England (New York: Berg, 2003).

diffusion of silk consumption.[27] By regulating luxury, the court aimed to stabilize status display and more importantly, the politics of dressing.[28] As the aristocracy gradually lost its hold on state power, clothing grew in significance as a self-fashioning tool for old and new elites alike.

Records of sartorial impropriety illustrate that Tang women defined their tastes outside of the prescribed ideal and produced an unstable yet fashionable world where "the aristocrats and the common people lack distinction." The breakdown of distinction between the aristocrats and the commoners embodied the move from fashion-as-material to fashion-as-social. This shift, whereby luxury fabrics were no longer reserved for the bodies of the aristocratic courtier, coupled with the privileging of personal taste over decorum, was evidence of the decaying empire. The desire to own and wear luxury silks according to one's own taste now fueled fashion.

Conclusion

Although laws governing dress continued to be promulgated until the collapse of the Tang dynasty in 907, they were consistently transgressed. The clamor of the officials' scrutiny of elite dressing reveals the significant space fashion inhabited in the court – a space that was repeatedly gendered female. Commentary on women's dress in the "Treatise on Carriages and Dress," the wealth of female representations in tombs, and the poetic associations of women's bodies with silk together suggest that Tang women were the agents of fashion. One reason for this may be that because men held public roles, their modes of dress were more firmly prescribed than women's dress. This public/private dichotomy may have allowed women to transgress prescription and proscription, while simultaneously making them targets of official censure.[29]

---

27 The three dominant regions of Tang silk production were the Yellow River region, consisting of modern Hebei and Henan provinces, followed by the Sichuan region, and the area south of the Yangtze River. The region of the Yangtze River grew in significance after the An Lushan rebellion of 755. The peripheral areas in the northwest of the empire were also important sites of production due to their proximity to the Silk Road trade routes. Zhao Feng, Zhongguo sichou tongshi [The General History of Chinese Silk], (Suzhou: Suzhou daxue chubanshe, 2005), 187-191.

28 The Byzantine silk industry and sumptuary legislation form an interesting parallel to the Tang. Scholarship has shown that the hierarchy of clothing proposed by the state was repeatedly undermined by the elites who could afford to purchase or pay for the illicit manufacturing of extravagant silks. See R.S. Lopez, "Silk Industry in the Byzantine Empire," Speculum 20 (1945): 1-42. Also see G.C. Maniates, "Organization, Market Structure, and Modus Operandi of the Private Silk Industry in Tenth-Century Byzantium," Dumbarton Oaks Papers 53 (1999): 263-332.

29 See Diana O. Hughes, "Regulating Women's Fashion," in A History of Women: Silences of the Middle Ages, Christiane Klapisch-Zuber, ed. (Cambridge: Harvard University Press, 1992), 136-58. Also, Catherine K. Killerby, Sumptuary Law in Italy 1200-1500 (New York: Clarendon, 2002).

The palace woman functioned as a trope in poetry as embodiments of the dynasty's excess, male desire, and the luxury silk market. As objects of the gaze, their visibility was central to the Tang fashion system. Their transgressions, validated by being observed and imitated, suggested a new sense of the clothed self that exceeded the order of fashion-as-material.

The emergence of fashion and an awareness of the phenomenon during the Tang dynasty grew out of two interrelated processes: the friction between a need for stable status display and a growing self-fashioning impulse catalyzed by social and economic change. In the seventh century, the courting of exotic accoutrements signaled a break from the idealized sartorial behavior exposing a desire to dress fashionably. This urge to play the fashion game spread through the course of the eighth century as trade filtered new styles into the wardrobe of the Tang woman. By the ninth century, changes in the Tang economic and political structure enabled the rise of a new fashionable elite whose politics of appearance was no longer dictated by the old symbolic order, but by the luxury silk economy. Fashion gained a wider audience, but it remained a practice reserved for the elite.

Figure 1. Mural of female attendant from the tomb of Prince Zhang Huai (706 CE). (Qianling Museum, Shaanxi Province)

Figure 2. Figure of a female horse rider sporting the popular *weimao*, excavated from the tomb of Zheng Rentai (664 CE). (Shaanxi History Museum, Xi'an)

Drawing Borders: Perceptions of the Cultural Other in Renaissance Costume Books

Gabriele Mentges

The Early Modern Period in Europe (the end of the 15th century and the 16th century) was a key period in the development of anthropological knowledge and scientific. It was also a time of great expansion of trade with distant countries and continents. New luxury items—such as spices, new fabrics, precious jewels, metal, furs, carpets, ceramics, and dyes—and new technologies for the production of glass, metal, and ceramics made their way to Europe from these far-off places. Historians recognize this trading system as the first global network of trade and cultural exchange.[1]

Can the first traces of orientalist thought and practice as formulated by Edward Said be found during the development of this global network in the Early Renaissance?

Said's understanding of Orientalism as an academic concept and method of dominance is based on military conquest, the establishment of administrative structures and infrastructures, and the formation of knowledge about the conquered Arab and Asian societies during the 19th century. For this reason, it may appear questionable whether the concept of Orientalism can be applied to the Early Renaissance, a time period far removed from the systematic conquering and colonisation that occurred in the 19th century and from the associations of power and knowledge that were necessarily coupled with these processes.[2]

But what if we instead ask whether and how a relationship between the Early Renaissance and the Orientalism of the 19th century could be constructed, or why clothing plays such a large role in engagements with other cultures? These questions are indeed legitimate.

In her most recently published book, *Dressing Up*, the historian Ulinka Rublack uses several different sources to analyse the enormous social significance that was attributed to clothing during the Renaissance in Europe. She reaches the clear and unambiguous conclusion that "'Western' fashion, quite simply, was invented in dialogue with the East […] display of taste and fashion was a cross-cultural phenomenon."[3] Even though Rublack's conclusion

---

[1] Jürgen Osterhammel / Niels P. Petterson: Geschichte der Globalisierung. Dimensionen, Prozesse, Epochen. Munich, Beck 2003, p. 39; Alexander Engel: Farben der Globalisierung. Die Entstehung moderner Märkte für Farbstoffe 1500-1900. Frankfurt am Main and New York, Campus 2009, pp. 51-61.
[2] I am referring to: Edward W. Said: Orientalism. Western Conceptions of the Orient. London, New York, Penguin 1995 (5th ed.).
[3] Ulinka Rublack: Dressing Up. Cultural Identity in Renaissance Europe. Oxford, Oxford University Press 2010, pp. 7-8.

has significant implications for the question posed at the beginning of this essay, it does not explain how processes of cultural exchange occurred, and it does not address whether there existed an aesthetic hegemony in the perception and appropriation of other cultural clothing artefacts that led to a dominant concept of representation.[4]

The following essay is an attempt to use the costume books of the Renaissance to explain how foreign—here defined as non-European and especially non-Western European—clothing cultures were represented and perceived.

The term "costume books" refers to a group of sources published between 1562 and 1600 that contain illustrations of costumes that appeared above all in Western Europe.[5] They contain illustrations of clothing worn around the world

---

4 The evidence that Rublack uses to support her arguments is most interesting. She uses the example of the North Indian Moguls, in which conspicuous consumption of clothing was one of the principle techniques of dominance. As C. A. Bayly demonstrated in his detailed analysis of historical clothing practices in North India, there were characteristic trains of pre-modern consumption behaviours among Mogul leaders—that could make them an exception. C.A. Bayly: The origins of swadeshi (home industry): cloth and Indian society, 1700-1930. In: Arjun Appudarai (ed.): The social life of things. Commodities in cultural perspective. Cambridge et al, Cambridge University Press 6, 2008, pp. 285-322.

5 The following books referred to here can be found in the Lipperheidische Kostümbibliothek (Lipperheidische Costume Library): 1562 Recueil de la diversité des habits qui sont de present en usage tant es pays d'Europe, Asie, Affrique&Isles sauvages. Erscheinungsort: Paris: Richard Breton / 2nd edition 1567, engraved by Enea Vico; 1563 Ferdinando Bertelli: Omnium fere gentium nostrae aetatis habitus... ; Place of publication: Venice. 60 sheet-sized engravings, probably by Enea Vico; 1572 Omnium fere gentium nostraeque aetatis nationum habitus&effiges. Antwerp. (copy of the publication from 1562); 1577 Abraham Bruyn: Omnium poene gentium imagines. 1578 ders: Imperii ac sacerdotii ornatus. Diversarum item gentium peculiaris vestitus (both volumes appear combined: 1581 and 1610); 1577 Hans Weigel: Habitus Praeciporum Populorum, tamvirorum quamfeminarum Singulari arte depicti (= Trachtenbuch: Darin fast allerley und der fürnembsten Nationen/die heutigs tags bekandt sein/kleidungen/beyde wie'es bey Manns und Weibspersonen gebreuchlich, mit allem vleiß abgerissen sein/sehr lustig und kurzweilig zusehen. Gedruckt zu Nürnberg/bey Hans Weigel Formschneider. Nürnberg; 1581 Habitus variarum orbis gentium. Habitz de nations estrages. Trachten mancherley Völcker des Erdskreysz. (Artist who probably produced many of the images: Jean Jacques Boissard: Boissard; 1585 Grassi Romano: Die veri ritratti degl' habiti di tutte le parti del mondo. Rom. ; 1585 Jost Ammann: Geistliches Trachtenbuch: Ordenstrachten, geistliche Trachten; 1586 ders. Frauenzimmer. Similar to Weigel's, but it is assumed that Amman worked independently from Weigel because, for one thing, many new costumes appear. Was inspired by Weigel and used Boissard as a model for the Italian costumes, and attributions of the clothing were apparently not important to him: he labels a woman from Florence as a Frenchwoman; 1590 Cesare Vecellio: Degli habiti antichi et moderni di diverse parti del mondo, Erscheinungsort: Venedig. 1598: 2nd edition, 3. 1664, Spanish translation 1794, 1859 u. 1860 new edition in Paris, which became famous because many of its drawings were attributed to Titian. Features of this work: more comprehensive: 1st edition: 418 woodcuts of costumes with many notes that contain important information about the culture. Images partially independently produced

as it was known at that point, including Central European trading centres—including Moscow and Turkey—and the Oriental and even the African world. They also address cultural groups that were known at the time, such as the Moors. They were the descendants of the Arab conquerors and made up a significant portion of the population in southern Spain and would later be driven out of the country.

The different types of clothing are classified primarily according to location, social standing (from maidservants, farmers, townswomen, and courtesans to wealthy patricians), and the wearer's stage in life as well as by the occasions for which they were worn, including weddings, holidays, and mourning. Research generally addresses about 12 of these books.[6]

These publications appear to disappear at the beginning of the 17th century, only to reappear again and in greater numbers at the end of the century and even more so in the 18th and 19th centuries.[7]

Until this point, academic interest in costume books has recognized them as being part of a body of knowledge of the Early Renaissance that is relevant to particular topics such as forms of clothing, representation of Indians, etc. However, they have not yet been treated as sources with multiple levels of meaning of their own.[8]

Not insignificantly, questions about the concept and construction of a united Europe seem to be kindling interest in this knowledge medium of the Early Renaissance.

---

by him: Venice, Terra ferma (his home), Dalmation region of Venice, and apart from that there is much borrowed from Boissard, Weigel, Grassi; 1589-1596 Pietro Bertelli: Diversarum nationum habitus. Patavii . Three volumes. 1. volume; 1589 illustrations above all pertaining to Venice, Padua, Northern Italy apparently independently produced but others are copies of previous illustrations (Bruyn, Weigel, Grassi, Boissard).

6 I am using the list of books that appeared in the exhibition organized by Walther (Walther, Rolf: Das Danziger Frauentrachtenbuch von Anton Moeller und seine Vorläufer im 16. Jahrhundert. In: Ernst Bahr (ed.): Studien zur Geschichte des Preußenlandes. Festschrift für Erich Kayser, Marburg Elwert Verlag 1963, pp.447-469).

7 The lack of interest in costum books in the 17th century requires further research. One possible explanation could be that this form of knowledge was presented in the fine arts until the logic of clothing was rediscovered. That was the case in the late 18th century and even more so in the following century.

8 See Isabel Paresys: Images de L'Autre vêtu à la Renaissance. Le recueil d'habits de François Desprez (1562-1567). In: Journal de la Renaissance Volume IV, 2006, pp. 25-56, for this issue, p.26. „Néanmoins les recueils d'habits attendent encore leur historien." From the point of view of a German speaker, this conclusion needs to be qualified. The beginnings of a thorough examination can be found in Doege, Heinrich: Die Trachtenbücher des 16. Jahrhunderts. In: Beiträge zur Bücherkunde und Philologie. Leipzig 1903, pp. 429-444. See also Walther, Op.Cit.

The first person in German-speaking regions to address this matter was Hans Doege.[9] Doege's meticulous research on image sources has provided precise and concrete evidence about the sources that were used for the images that appear in the books, about plagiarism of images, and about great inaccuracies in the labelling of costumes and places. Doege also pays attention to the character of the costume books as a new knowledge medium in the Early Renaissance: he recognizes that they are attempts at a scientific compilation of material culture relationships and connections even as he laments their arbitrariness and lack of taxonomic organisation. Among their deficiencies, he names the books' false attributions of costume and place and multiple incidences of image plagiarism. In light of the few reliable pieces of information and of the lack of scientific classification (arbitrariness) that is familiar to us today and that Doege bemoaned, it is not surprising that he reaches the conclusion that the costume books cannot be used for research on dress cultures. Rolf Walther later made the same critical remarks about this body of sources.[10]

For Doege and Walther, the costume book genre reaches its definitive conclusion with the Danzig Costume Book by Anton Moeller in 1601. He produced this book using city books, like those by Georg Braun and Franz Hogenberg, and the hand-drawn costume book of Sigmund Heldt from Nuremburg (1565-1567) as models. According to Walther, at this point there is a shift from universal to local focus. In addition to the local orientation, a realistic mode of costume representation comes to the fore. This mode of representation testifies to immediate observation and empathy—"out of the statutory isolation of the figures [ensues] their physical and spatial unification in scenes, the meticulous observation of costumes details, whose combination results in the effects of fabrics and movements" .

---

9 Walther, op. cit. See David Gilbert: Urban outfitting: The City and the Spaces of Fashion Cultures. In: Stella Bruzzi (ed.): Fashion Cultures. Theories, Explorations and Analysis. London/New York, Routledge 2000, pp. 7-24. More specific information on the significance of the relation between the city and clothing can be found in: Christopher Breward/David Gilbert (ed.): Fashion's World Cities. Oxford/New York, Berg 2006.

10 Walther, op. cit. A later continuation of this approach, though revised using modern methods, is the exclusively art historical research of Susanne Förg, whose value will not be contested here but which nonetheless contains no cultural historical perspectives. See: „Die Bilderhandschrift (1580) aus der Lipperheideschen Kostümbibliothek." Unpublished Master's Thesis from the Humbold-Universität, Berlin 1998. The study addresses the costume book „Trachtenbuech. Darinen viller Volckher ynnd Nationen Claidung vnnd zier begrüffen weliche nit allain lustig zu sechen, Sondern auch Nutzlich zue aller zier zu gebrauchen Mit groser mühe vnnd arbait zuesamen getragen vor Nie gesechenn volendet", Anno 1580. Primo May.

Walther references important changes: the quantitative increase of the illustrations of female persons and a shift in spatial perception that is still related to emblematic art yet demonstrates new continuity of space.[11]

Even if his one-sided fixation on the problems posed by the sources obstructs his ability to see other levels of meaning particular to costume books, Walther's discussion of space anticipates new current research perspectives on the books. First of all, he pays attention to the relationship between space, the body, costume, and techniques of representation. Secondly, he alludes to the relationship between space and gender. And lastly, he notes the changes in the construction and perception of space brought about by social and cultural processes.

The term "costume books" is understood more broadly in the following essay. In contrast to older research,[12] it is not limited to the costume books that were edited as was customary but instead also draws upon illustrated writings, such as those by Christoph Weiditz (1532)[13] and Sigmund Heldt.[14]

The costume books convey knowledge about the cultural Other primarily through their visual representations, which constitute the majority of the books.[15] In spite of the recognizable appropriation of image motifs and the similarity of many illustrations, this body of sources cannot be treated as a uniform entity. It is rather the case that the individual books form different discourses and develop their own patterns of meaning. Through their mutual citation and transformation of images, they create an intermedial network whose modified, appropriated motifs allude to changed perspectives in image-based discourse about the Other.[16] How are the books used to construct a relationship to the cultural Other? Do they constitute the mechanism of an Early Renaissance "orientalist discourse"?

---

11 Walther, op. cit., p. 461
12 Doege, Hans: Die Trachtenbücher des 16. Jahrhunderts. In: Beiträge zur Bücherkunde und Philologie. Leipzig. 1903, pp. 429-444.
13 Weiditz Christoph: Das Trachtenbuch des Christoph Weiditz von seinen Reisen nach Spanien (1529) und den Niederlanden ((1531-32). Nürnberg Ca 1532. Reprinted in Berlin, DeGruyter 1975 (after the manuscript preserved in the library of the National Museum in Nuremberg).
14 Heldt, Sigmund: Heldt'sches Trachtenbuch. Abcontairfaittung allerlei ordenspersonen in iren klaidungen und dan viler alter klaidungen, so vor zeiten von Fursten, #Furstin nd herrn, auch Burger und Burgerin, alhie zu Nuremberg und vilen andern orten getragen sinnt worden Nürnberg 1560-80. Ort. Lipp Aa2
15 The fashion journals of the 19th century operate in a different manner. See the essay by Gertrud Lehnert.
16 See Rublack op. cit., p. 148. She emphasizes the differences among the books. See Gabriele Mentges: Vestimentäres Mapping. Trachtenbücher und Trachtenhandschriften des 16. Jahrhunderts. In: Waffen- und Kostümkunde. vol. 46 2004, nr.1, pp. 28-29.

Clothing, Bodies, and Space

As a popular knowledge medium of the Early Renaissance that had a Western European readership, the costume books are part of the knowledge being collected at the time. They are also part of an ethnological body of knowledge that was being constituted in a very specific way. What is special about the books is that they create a relationship between body and clothing and space in which, according to Grimes, the Western European perspective is expressed. That also explains their use as rhetoric devices in contemporary cartography.[17] Grimes's argument is supported by the detailed and productive research done by Isabelle Paresys. According to Paresys, the costumed figures that appear on many maps and that at first appear to be decorative figures in the tradition of emblematic art have their own levels of meaning.[18] The costumed figures were added for multiple reasons: they were signs of urbanity, they conveyed a certain bearing and "postume," and they helped illustrate and didactically support the statements that were made—which provided an advantage on the competitive market.[19]

The "costume figures" do not only contribute to the perception and construction of space in maps. The costume book genre as a whole conveys its own perception of space and produces cultural orders of space that refer to geographical regions. The orientation towards the human figure, its size, and the creation of its outward appearance using clothing create a different concept of space than the one that the maps could convey. This particularity arises due to the structuring effect of the clothing: it instructs using poses, gestures, and the taste of the urban elite; it identifies social hierarchies; and it informs about the cultural differences that can be perceived through dress. Cultural differences related to places and spaces are made clear by the clothing and clothed bodies. Not only does space become concrete and tangible; this method of representation also trains empirical seeing, understanding, and description.[20]

---

17 See for this aspect Kristen Ina Grimes: Dressing the World. Costume Books and Ornamental Cartography in the Age of Exploration. In: Elizabeth Rodini/ Elissa B. Weaver (Hrsg.): A Well-Fashioned Image. Clothing and Costume in European Art, 1500-1850. Chicago, University of Chicago Press 2002, S. 12-21. Grimes' study is based on 2 costume books (Vecellio 1590, und Omnium fere gentium nostraeque 1572 anonymus) as well as on 2 maps of the 16th. century. p.14.

18 See as examples the famous and well known book of maps by Braun & Hogenberg Civitates Orbis Terrarum Köln, 1. Band ab 1572, and also the atlas Novus von Jonan Willem Blaeue (Amsterdam, since 1635)

19 Isabelle Paresys: Apparences vestimentaires et cartographie de l'espace en Europe occidentale aux XVIè et XVIIè siècle. In: Dies. (Hrsg.) : Paraître et apparences en Europe occidentale du Moyen Age à nos jours, Villeneuve d'Ascq, Septentrion 2008. S.253-270.

20 See Mentges 2004 op. cit., pp. 19-36., here pp. 31-32. For more on the relationship of space and clothing, see : Pour une approche renouvelée des recueils de costumes de la Renaissance. Une cartographie vestimentaire de l'espace et du temps, in Apparence(s), Nr.1:

This affinity between clothing and space applies particularly to the city. Specifics about the setting are not clear in the image but rather are described in the text; thus language's power of description and its relationship to images plays an important role.[21]

Eugenia Paulicelli brings an additional perspective on costume books into play when she claims that the final costume book by Cesare Vecellio, "Degli/habiti/antichi, et/moderni/di diversi Parti del Mondo", can be considered the precursor to fashion magazines. The similarly weighted design, text, and images of the costume book supports such an association, as do the references make to clothing producers and production methods.[22]

L'autre vêtu: The clothed Other

The "clothed Other", a term that appears in the title of Isabelle Paresys' essay, is another central issue pertaining to these books. The costume books address the issue of the Other in two manners: they treat Others as unhuman beings and monsters and represent them as a cultural Other—Africans, Moors, Tartars, and especially Indians, that Other of all Others.[23]

In Desprez's Récueil of 1562 there are monsters that are represented in the medieval tradition, but their representations include other nuances and

---

http://apparences.revues.org/104 [last access 04.12.2012]. Also see : Mentges 2003: Fashion, Time and the Consumption of a Renaissance Man in Germany : The Costume Book of Matthäus Schwarz in Augsburg 1496-1564. In: Barbara Burman/Carole Turbin : Material Strategies. Dress and Gender in Historical Perspective. Malden/Oxford/Melbourne : Blackwell 12-33.

21 Mentges 2004, pp. 31-32. The significant trade centres of the Renaissance were well-poised to gloat about their ability to clothe their citizens well. Clothing was a significant and costly trading good that created relationships between spaces and that was often the foundation that the wealth of cities was built upon. For more this matter today, see David Gilbert: Urban outfitting: The City and the Spaces of Fashion Cultures. In: Stella Bruzzi (Hrsg.): Fashion Cultures. Theories, Explorations and Analysis. London/New York, Routledge 2000, pp. 7-24. More more specific information on the relationship between cities and clothing, see: Christopher Breward/David Gilbert (Hrsg.): Fashion's World Cities. Oxford/New York, Berg 2006.

22 Eugenia Paulicelli: Mapping the world. The political geography of dress in Cesare Vecellios Costume Book. In: The Italienist. Journal of the Departments of Italian Studies, University of Reading et Al.. 28 (2008) 1, pp. 24-53. Paulicelli produces a very thorough interpretation of Vecellio's book, in which she emphasizes his relation with the tradition of civilité. We cannotm however, accept all aspects of Paulicelli's method of interpretation. Her argument that Vecellio's book exercises memory techniques lacks the proper foundations. She also appears to have no difficult projecting modern categorical concepts upon the Renaissance, such as when she uses the term "national styles" on p. 27.

23 See Jean Ceard / Jean-Claude Margolin: Voyager à la Renaissance. In: Voyager à la Renaissance. Actes du colloque de Tours 30 Juin-13 Juillet 1983, sous la direction de Jean Ceard et de Jean-Claude Margolin, Paris, Éditions Maisonneuve et Larose 1987, pp. 9-34, p.14. „C'est l'Autre, celui dont ni les Anciens grécolatins ni la Bible n'évoquait la présence...".

overtones, such as the mockery of the clergy. In the other books, the cultural Other appears with varying frequency and in other forms, numerically lead by the Turks.[24] In the literature, it is widely agreed-upon that the initial European finding of the self and drawing of borders takes place at this time. Through this process, the cultural self-reflection discussed by Mario Erdheim developed.[25]

The eurocentric perspective of ethnography at the time is not contested, but its unique aim was not, as M. Hodgen maintains, to celebrate European superiority. Instead, it was also a means of looking critically at the European population or of expressing hidden criticism of moral conditions.[26]

"A Visual Cacaphony"? Costume Books as Knowledge Medium and Space of Knowledge

The characteristics described above demonstrate to what extent the "costume books" were also an important archive of ethnological information.

In Margaret T. Hodgen's account of Early Renaissance ethnology,[27] the books are addressed as ethnographic delineations. Even though costume books are not discussed in great depth, Hodgen's basic ruminations on the knowledge media of the Early Renaissance are interesting. In contrast to the rather harsh—but from contemporaries' standpoint understandable—judgments made by Doege,

---

24 See Metropolitan Museum of Art (ed.): Venice and the Islamic World 828-1797. New York, New Haven and London. Yale University Press, 2007. The intense trading relationships between Venice and the Ottoman Court during the 16th century (ca. 1453-1571) spurred on this particular interest and lead to lively, mutual interaction, including the stay of the painter Gentile Bellini (1479) at the Ottoman Court, where he produced portraits of the Turkish Sultan and his dignitaries. See especially the chapter "The Serenissima and the Sublime Port: Art in the Art of Diplomacy 1453-1600", p. 107. The catalog also references notworthy characteristics of the Early Renaissance "globalization", such as cheap copies of "oriental artefacts" and the reimportation of inexpensive cotton in Egypt, the latter of which caused a decline in prices there, etc.

25 See Blanc op. cit., Mentges op. cit. 2004, Mentges op.cit. 2006, Paresys op. cit. 2006; on self-reflection, see: Mario Erdheim: Anthropologische Modelle des 16. Jahrhunderts. In: Wolfgang Marschall (ed.): Klassiker der Kulturanthropologie. Munich, Beck 1990, pp. 19-50.

26 See Paresys op. cit. 2006, p.48: Criticism expressed by Francois Desprez (among others) was aimed against courtiers and the Church. See also Nicole Pellegrin: Vêtements de peau(x) et de plumes: la nudité des indiens et la diversité du monde au XVIème siècle. In : Jean Céard/ Jean-Claude Margolin (eds.): Voyager à la Renaissance. Paris, Maisonneuve et Larose 1987, pp. 509-546. Pellegrin emphasizes differences in the gaze garments when garments are concerned. Also see Kirsten Mahlke: Indianer und Narren. Zur karnevalesken Rezeption von Jean de Lérys Histoire d'un voyage fait en la terre du Brésil. In: Renate Schlesier / Ulrike Zellmann (eds.): Reisen über Grenzen. Kontakt und Konfrontation, Maskerade und Mimikry. Münster, Waxmann 2003, pp. 101-119. Relevant here is p. 105. Playing with ones own people and with the Other became "serious societal criticism" under the influence of Calvinism.

27 See: Early Anthropology in the Sixteenth and Seventeenth Century. Pennsylvania, University of Pennsylvania Press 1998 (1. A. 1964).

Hodgen recognizes that the different authors were aware of the need to develop a scholarly method of their own, even if they, in the end, chose a traditional solution to the dilemma by returning to traditional sources and patterns of explanation. The desire to present the reading public of the Renaissance with ethnological data clearly through descriptions and to convey it entertainingly using categories such as food, religion, family, clothing, ritual, etc. created unprecedented intellectual and other challenges for the authors; these issues were different from those involved in previous artefact collecting practices. On the one hand, in the light of current research on the history of collecting, Margaret Hodgen's work can no longer be accepted in its entirety; but on the other, the notion that the complexity of the ethnological information required a different scholarly method than other collections of artefacts being built at the time raises the question of the contribution of material artefacts like clothing and the techniques of their representation to the history of ethnological knowledge.

An in-depth investigation of the sartorial dimension also leads to a re-evaluation of the lack of classification that has been mentioned time and again since Heinrich Doeges's work was published.[28] Clothing, as part of material culture, offers us a category of observation, and one that—if carefully formulated—offers the possibility of impartial observations. The clothing obliges us to engage in an empirical form of seeing that has not been commonly practiced, and the descriptions oblige us to undertake a similar analysis of the written component of the books.[29] Through the compilation and visual ordering of the individual images of clothing, the books emerged as a new form of conveying knowledge, one that could be reproduced and published using new printing techniques.

In her detailed analysis of Francois Desprez's first costume book from 1562, the "Recueil des Costumes", Isabelle Paresys proved that, contrary to the widely-held assumption that the book is a "visual cacaphony", it is actually arranged according to visual critera: it is grouped according to pairs (man and woman) who appear across from each other. Desprez deals with various differences in clothing in a similar manner. He does not arrange costumes

---

28 Also see Nicole Pellegrin: Ordre et désordres des images. Les représentations et les classifications des costumes régionaux d'Ancien Régime. In: L'Ethnographie 1984, pp. 387-400. Odile Blanc takes a similar position (la cohérence sans genre) in her essay „Images du monde et portraits d'habits: les recueils de costumes à la Renaissance. In: Bulletin du bibliophile 2, 1995, pp. 221-261, here p. 224 ff. Both have the benefit of approaching the books from a modern perspective.

29 Vgl. Mentges op. cit., 2004, wird in diesem Fall für die Handschrift von Weiditz vertreten, der ihrer Ansicht als Teil des Quellenkorpus betrachtet werden sollte, wenngleich nur als Handschrift bekannt, S. 27-28; vgl. Theodor Hampe (Hg.): Das Trachtenbuch des Christoph Weiditz von seinen Reisen nach Spanien (1529) und den Niederlanden (1531-32). Berlin/Leipzig, de Gruyter 1927. 2001 wurde ein Faksimile des Trachtenbuchs in Spanien veröffentlicht. „El Códices de trajes. Faksimile, 2. Bde., Valencia, 2001.

according to geographical location or meaning but rather according to the visual effect of the clothing: that is why the lightly clothed inhabitants of Provence are situated across from the warmly clothed Poles. This form of ordering confirms that representations of the "clothed Other" play an important role in this book.

A further ordering mechanism is the geographical position of the author. Desprez's geographical system begins at his own location and proceeds further afield; he first describes what appears in his region and what he knows best. The level of detail of the descriptions corresponds to his knowledge.[30]

In addition to their ethnological aspects, modern research emphasizes the importance of the costume books as knowledge media; Odile Blanc in particular recognizes this quality.[31] The space of the book necessitates a specific form of representation. Eugenia Paulicelli has discovered a most particular form of representation in Vecellio's costume book; according to her, it contains a spatial dimension: it is conceived as a palace whose rooms are visited by the reader. In this regard, the book has the character of a portable museum.[32]

If we push Paulicelli's arguments further, we can argue that the books also have the character of imaginary collections of clothing. This identification is appropriate on multiple levels. First, on the level of formal design, the arrangement of the first books as observed by Blanc is essentially a collection of loose sheets that were later bound together, which lent coherence to the visual aspects of the books. The process of production also resembles collecting, but representations of objects are collected instead of the tangible objects themselves. It is for this reason that Nicole Pellegrin sees a relationship between contemporary cabinets of curiosity and the books, even though they both have their own specificities.[33]

In this manner, the books become public places in which the Western European rules of clothing and corporeality are explicitly laid out for the first time. Rublack notices this in Hans Weigels costume book (1577), which she interprets as a bourgeois model of propriety with patriotic interests.[34]

Through cultural comparisons and their implicit values, the books also express power relationships developing between the European West and the cultural Other.

The format of knowledge used in the illustrated book leads us to ask in what way aesthetic processes participated in the construction of knowledge about the

---

30 See Mentges op. cit., 2004, p. 30.
31 Odile Blanc: „Images du monde et portraits d'habits: les recueils de costumes à la Renaissance. In: Bulletin du bibliophile 2, 1995, pp. 221-261, here p. 228.
32 Paulicelli op. cit. 2008, p. 30, pp. 40-41.
33 See Pellegrin op. cit. 1987, p. 529 and Daniel Defert: Les collections iconographiques du XVIème siècle. In Jean Ceard / Jean-Claude Margolin op.cit.1987, p. 51.
34 See Rublack op.cit 2010, p. 161.

cultural Other.³⁵ What is special about this particular knowledge medium in comparison to the many travel books that were published? How is it constructed through relationships to the cultural Other? Could it be part of an Early Renaissance orientalist discourse?

The overall absence of clothing and fashions from India and China is striking and surprising in light of India's immense significance as a valued trading partner of Western Europeans.

"Orientalized" Themes of the Costume Books

Different themes suggest a relationship to preliminary thought processes of an early "Orientalism." First of all, there are the rich and varied representations of the Ottoman Empire, and then there are also the various forms of clothing worn in Africa, Arabia, Southern Europe, the North, and the Northeast. The clothing worn by the Tartars and the inhabitants of the New World, as well as veiling, are also depicted. These vestimentary topographies appear regularly, though they are treated and arranged differently by different authors. These pictorial representations, as well as their transformations and placement, will be analysed in the following sections with special attention to the statements they make about the Other and to question of whether they constitute the first orientalist discourse.

Ottoman Fashion

There is an impressive variety of illustrations of the fashion of the Ottoman Empire.³⁶ Corresponding travel literature was produced in parallel. Europeans appear to have been fascinated with the luxury of the Ottoman Court and the diversity of the clothing worn there—especially the clothing of the Ottoman dignitaries and women with their foreign sartorial practices and rituals.

In a certain regard, the Ottoman culture of appearances was very similar to the one operating in Europe. Near the end of the 16th century, the Moroccan Ambassador Abu-I-Hasan El-Tamgruti reported that there were strict, hierarchical vestimentary rules at the Ottoman Court. Precise observation of sartorial details informed the foreign visitor about the class and function of his interlocutor.³⁷

---

35 This question is formulated with reference to Peter Geimers "Ordnungen der Sichtbarkeit". Peter Geimers: Ordnungen der Sichtbarkeit. Frankfurt am Main, Suhrkamp Publishing 2002, p. 8.

36 "The rise of the Ottoman Empire was due to the conquest by Iranian nobles who occupied Anatolia – Il Khaniden – first emperor of the Mamluks, the empire stretching from Egypt to Syria from 1250 until 1517 and became the principal trading partner of the Venetian Republic." Metropolitan Museum of Art op. cit., 2007, p. 73.

37 Abou-I-Hasan Ali ben Mohammed El-Tamgrouti: Relation d'une ambassade marocaine en Turquie 1589-1591. Translation by Henri de Castres, Paris 1929, p. 61, cited by

Above all, the Ottoman dignitaries impressed the Europeans with the high turbans that they wore as status symbols. Europeans also marvelled at the elaborate headgear of the women and the lavish clothing, shoes and fabric, as well as the poses and forms of behaviour, even those of children, which were seldom seldom used to represent value. Head coverings played an extremely important role in the presentation of social status, rank, ethnicity, and religious belief in the Ottoman Empire.[38] Visitors also took note of women being transported on sedans under canopies.[39]

The illustrators' interest in the women appears to have been kindled less by their veiling practices than by their completely different way of dressing, behaving, and moving.[40] Unveiled women were also shown. The discourse on veiling in the Ottoman Empire only became politically virulent after the beginning of colonization and through encounters with West since the 18th century. Clothing ordonances issued by the Sultan at the time drew new boundaries between Muslim natives and Christian foreigners.[41]

The more or less equal consideration of the sexes in the illustrations suggests that the male illustrators were not particularly interested in an orientalizing femininity. The illustrations rather convey a neutral, factual impression.[42] Whether Pietro Bertelli's illustration of a bride in a sedan, whom the visitor can see by lifting the veil of the bridal tent (a piece of paper glued onto the image), is an exception to this rule is questionable[43] because it could also be a factual representation and a testimony to European curiosity.

Contemporary travel literature, however, indicates the opposite: travel books were explicitly interested in the Ottomans' particular way of interacting with women, who were largely withdrawn from public spaces. This discrepancy between the media of image and text draws attention to the different possibilities

---

Suraiya Faroqhi: L'histoire du costume ottoman. Un petit bilan de recherche. In: Marie Viallon (Hg.), Paraître et se vêtir au XVIè siècle., Saint-Etienne 2006, p. 96.

38 See Turba Kurtulus: Höfische Kopfbedeckungen der Osmanen. In: Deniz Erduman-Calis (ed.): Tulpen, Kaftane und Levni. Höfische Mode und Kostümalben aus dem Topkapi Palast Istanbul. Katalog zur gleichnamigen Ausstellung im Museum für Angewandte Kunst Frankfurt 14.10. 2008-11.1.2009 Munich 2008, pp. 192-203, here p. 192.

39 Travel literature reflects explicit interested in the veiling of the women, though without criticism. See Nils Büttner: Die "Turckische Frawe und ihr Bad". In: Ulrike Ilg (ed.): Text und Bild in Reiseberichten des 16. Jahrhunderts. Westliche Zeugnisse über Amerika und das osmanische Reich. Venice 2008, pp. 95-133, here p. 105-106.

40 However, some authors maintain precisely the opposite. See, for example, Büttner, op. cit 2008, pp. 105-106.

41 See Kurtulus op. Cit. 2008, p. 194 and p. 197 on the clothing reform of Mahmud II. in 1829. During the 19th century, Western influences were incorporated into fashion.

42 Büttner concurs. Büttner op.cit. 2008, pp. 107-109. He note that the word "harem" does not appear at all and that it was only used in the following centuries.

43 See Büttner and note 31. It is not clear, however, if Büttner is referring to the bridal tent or to the sedan.

and freedoms inherent in each medium: texts could or were allowed to have more freedom while visual media still required empirical exactitude.

One of the most famous and most popular travel books, "Les quatre premiers livres de Navigations et Pérégrinations Orientales", was written by Nicolas de Nicolay. It was published for the first time in 1567 in Lyons, and many costume books refer to its impressions of places abroad.[44] Especially Vecellio's comparatively late costume book from 1590, "Degli habiti antichi et moderni di diverse parti del mondo", was influenced by Nicolay. Vecellio's book is voluminous and has the largest number of drawings, some of which have been attributed to Titian.[45] Other sources that Vecellio could have used are the costume books known as "registers" that Europeans wrote during the last quarter of the 16th century during visits to the Ottoman Empire. They contain rich descriptions of Ottoman clothing.[46] Vecellio's book certainly attests to this.

Vecellio's interest can be explained above all by the lively trade that the Venetian Republic carried out (all in all from 828 to 1797) with the Ottoman Empire. Venice was the hub of trade with the entire Orient, including Egypt. Textiles were especially popular trading goods, including the silk and rugs that were luxuries for the Europeans. However, neither the trade with the Ottoman and the Mamluk Empires [47] nor the cultural exchange had a particularly strong influence on Venetian and Italian fashion. It was rather the case that the oriental textiles were used to decorate homes and churches. The Venetians were the most important carpet traders in all of Europe. The portraits painted by many Venetian painters demonstrate the importance of oriental carpets in Venetian decoration.[48] However, trade in Eastern Mediterranean textiles began to decline as early as the 15th century.

---

44 E.g. Johann Theodor and Johann Israel de Bry, Acta Machmeti I Saracenorum principes, Frankfurt am Main 1597; Pierre Belon: Portraits d'oyseaux, animaux, serpens, herbes, arbres, hommes et femmes, d'Arabie & Eygypte (...), Paris 1557 etc. Ottoman clothing practices and recorded excellently in a series of woodcuts that was published in Antwerp in 1553. "Les Moeurs et façons de faire de Turcs", which had as a model the drawings of the Antwerpian painter and architect Pieter Coecke van Aelst (1502-1550). See Büttner op. cit., S. 103. Travel accounts of the Ottoman Court begin to appear in the first half of the 15th century. See Almut Höfert: Turcica: Repräsentative Reiseberichte. In: Ilg op. cit. 2008, pp. 38-94, p. 91.

45 1590 Cesare Vecellio: Degli habiti antichi et moderni di diverse parti del mondo. Venice, first edition 1598, third edition 1664, Spanish translation 1794, new editions in 1859 and 1860, Paris. For more on Vecellio, see Paulicelli op. cit. 2008, pp. 24-53.

46 Julian Raby: The Serenissima and the Sublime Porte: Art in the Art of Diplomacy 1453-1600. In: Metropolitan Museum of Art op. cit. 2007, pp. 91-119, p.113.

47 The Mamluk Empire stretched from Syria to Egypt near the Mediterranean Sea from 1215 to 1517. Deborah Howard: Venice and the Mamluks ", in: Metropolitan Museum of Art op.cit 2007, pp. 72-89, here p. 73.

48 Walter Denny: Oriental Carpets and Textiles in Venice,in: Venice and the Islamic World 828-1797 op. cit. 2007, pp.175-191, here pp. 178-179 and p. 181.

Trade in oriental textiles with Eastern and Central Europe, however, became extremely important—especially with Russia. In these regions, there had been great demand for Ottoman silks for both secular and sacred purposes since the middle of the 16th century.[49] When the Venetian painter Bellini was sent to the Ottoman Court at the end of the 14th century to paint portraits of the courtiers and the Sultan, he acquainted the Ottoman elite with Western ways of looking and representing the ideal. Although the Sultan was excited by the velvet clothing of the Venetian nobility, there was no great move to imitate European fashions and art. The same was not true of the Venetians, however: "Whereas Ottomans figured prominently in Vecellio's compendium (book VII was devoted to the Habiti dei Turchi), the Frankish component in the Ottoman costume books was comparatively small. For the Venetians, the Ottomans were the defining 'Other', the foreigners whose looming presence spurred reflection on Venetian identity. With their empire stretching in all directions, across the 'seven climes', and though Venice was a critical point in their perception of the West, the political, religious, and cultural horizons of the Ottomans lay predominantly in the East."[50]

The Ottomans' different perception of the Other can be partially explained by Islamic societies' relationship with figurative representations. However, it does not explain why they had no desire to imitate European fashion. If for the Europeans possessions—material culture—were the basis for constructing the self and way of acquiring the world as a "collecting of the self,"[51] it can be supposed that material culture was not associated with the same desire for expansion and possession in the Ottoman Empire. The Ottoman constitution of a cultural self appears, in this regard, not to have been dependant on material culture.[52]

Asia and Arabia: A Glance beneath the Clothing

The first considerable encounter with the clothing of the Other occurred in Spain, where, after the fall of the Caliphate in Cordoba in 1492 and the end of reconquisition, Islamic culture was able to survive under the tolerance of the Castilian kings. Christoph Weiditz recorded the Spanish Moors, Muslims who

---

49 Richard Ettinghausen makes a similar argument but neglects fashion completely. See Ettinghausen: Der Einfluss der Angewandten Künste und der Malerei auf die Künste Europas. In: Gereon Sievernich/ Hendrik Budde: Europa und der Orient 800-1900. Munich 1989, pp. 165-209.

50 See Metropolitan Museum of Art op. cit 2007, p. 113.

51 This formulation is from James Clifford: Sich selbst sammeln. In: Gottfried Korff/Martin Roth (eds.): Das historische Museum. Frankfurt/M./New York 1990: Campus, pp.87-106. If we consider the costume books to be collecting practices, then Cliffords definition of a "Western subjectivity" is appropriate here. p .92.

52 Research has hardly addressed this question partly due to a lack of relevant contemporary documents.

had converted to Christianity and who wore what Europeans considered unusual clothing, in his illustrated costume book of 1532.[53] His drawings are convincing owing to their ethnographic exactitude and richness of detail.[54] Weiditz recorded the costumes of many regions in Western Europe in his costume book; these were regions that he actually travelled. In Spain, he met the famous Admiral Andrea Doria from Genoa (1466-1560), who had brought back Indians from his travels. He was the first to produce illustrations of Indians with the same level of ethnographic detail as other persons. Many later illustrations of Indians were based on Weiditz's work. His watercolours of the Moors display an independant Arab clothing style, and, in contrast to the so-called later costume books, they illustrate scenes, such as the Moorish woman sweeping her house with her child. These also served as models for later costume books; however, the latter do not share Weiditz's unpartisan exactitude but rather transform the images to suit certain ideologies. Thus Weiditz's precisely drawn Moorish women appear in the work of Sigmundt Heldt (1560-70) and Bartolomeo Grassi (1581) with ventilated upper-body clothing and expose their naked breasts in a pose that the illustrator never would have been able to observe first-hand.[55]

Equally implausible, though with the same ease, European travellers boast about their knowledge of Ottoman baths for women and secret women's rooms.[56]

The sequence of portrayed persons and their Arabic/African heritage—the transitions between different regions, cities, and countries—appears fluid and rather arbitrary. Illustrations of people from Southeast Europe are followed by Ottomans, Syrians, Persians, Palestinians, oriental Jews, and even gypsies and Ethiopians are mentioned. The series of images closes with the black "Moors" from Africa. In many regards, their clothing is similar to that worn by the Europeans, although the footwear, drapery, and adornment of arms and legs are different, and, in radical contrast to the European women, the women are portrayed partially unclothed. Their posture and poses are reminiscent of those of Weiditz's Indians.

The method of representing Arab-African figures, which was the same in many costume books, contains cryptic elements of judgment by the European

---

53 For more on his biography and work, see Theodor (ed.): Das Trachtenbuch des Christoph Weiditz von seinen Reisen nach Spanien (1529) und den Niederlanden (1531/32). Berlin / Leipzig 1921. In the following, the American edition of Hampe will be used for information on Weiditz's work and bibliography: Authentic Everyday Dress of the Renaissance. 1994. References to the images, which Hampe comments upon extensively, are the same as in the German edition.
54 For an evaluation of Weiditz, see Mentges 2004, Rublack op. cit. 2010, p. 187.
55 Heldt op. cit.; Bartolomeo Grassi: Dei veri ritratti de gli habiti... Di tutte le parti del mondo... Rom 1585.
56 European travel reports mention Turkish women in baths, where travellers in all reality could not have seen the women. Büttner op. cit., pp. 109-111. In: Ulrike Ilg op. cit.

gaze. The cultural distance between the civilized Europeans and the distant Other is expressed through increasing nakedness. A new and shameless gaze is directed primarily at the female body, which is portrayed unsparingly. A different visual rule is applied to foreign men: the closer the men live to the Arab-African borders, the more warlike they appear and are portrayed with bows, arrows, and pelts tied about their waists. They also resemble the Indians portrayed by Weiditz. Abraham de Bruyn's costume book from 1577, "Omnium poene gentium imagines", describes them as warlike and aggressive.[57] This gradual assimilation of differences into a convention of viewing based on similarities demonstrates the extent to which initial differentiations in the gaze and looking can lead to unifying stereotyping.

People of the North

The route to the European North and Northeast lead through Prussia, Poland, and the lands of the warlike Tartars. *Muscovites* was the term that the books normally used to refer to inhabitants of the contemporary Russian Empire. Western Europeans noted what was to them the unusual, antiquated-looking clothing of the Russians, who wore splendid caftans in the Byzantine style and high fur hats. The decision of the Russian elite to wear Byzantine-style clothing was probably made during the 15th century. Until that time, they had conformed to the Western European style. The occasion for the change in fashion was apparently the wedding of Ivan III and the Byzantine princess Sophia. From that point on, fashion played an increasingly important role for Russia's national identity in relation to Europe.[58] Russia took on a special role for the Europeans not just because of clothing, however; there were also religious issues. Russia was considered as foreign in this regard as Constantinople, although it was actually a Christian land.

According to Michael Harbsmeier, people travelling in Russia faced the dilemma of turning either to the triangular cosmology, in which the Muscovites were treated like the Ottomans, or of turning to the new cosmologic vision that considered Russia to be an ignorant and uncivilized society. Whatever decision they made presented travellers with unresolvable difficulites. Many travel reports thus describe Russian behaviour and relations similarly to those of the Ottomans. However, in Russia there were no threats or attempts to convert travellers to the Islamic faith, which was characteristic of European travellers' relations with the Muslim Other.[59]

---

57 Bruyn op. cit. 1577: Ders.op. cit. 1578.
58 Reineking von Bock, Gisela: Die Kleidung in Russland zur Zeit der Romanovs. In: Gisela Reineking von Bock (ed.): Prunkvolles Zarenreich. Eine Dynastie blickt nach Westen 1613-1917. Cologne Publishers 2nd edition. 1997, pp. 82-93, pp. 82-84.
59 Michael Harbsmeier: Elementary Structures of Otherness. An Analysis of Sixteenth Century German Travel Accounts. In: Jean Ceard/Claude Margolin (ed.): Voyager à la Renaissance. Actes du Colloque de Tours 30 Juni – 13 Juli 1983, pp. 337-356 , pp. 347-348.

The fact that the costume books portray the social hierarchy of the Muscovite realm in detail suggests that they are using the same mode of perception that was also used for the Ottomans. The Muscovites remain similarly foreign. The Tartars, who are next in the sequence, are reduced to a warlike appearance and portrayed with arrows, bows, and the appropriate clothing. This method of depiction is overtly similar to the manner in which many Arab figures are portrayed. The word *Tartars* was used to refer to the Mongols, who, according to de Bruyn, were agressive barbarians threatening Europe.[60]

Here as well, the same process of combining distance and aggression is used to create an assessment category.

Inhabitants of the lands beyond the Black Sea are shown clothed entirely in pelts and peculiar head coverings. This form of clothing was already known in Antique Greece, where the so-called Scythians were portrayed on vases. This example demonstrates that the authors of the costume books used both old and new sources of images for their narrations.[61]

Veiling

Illustrations of Italian cities like Genoa, Venice, Padua, and Milan depict veiled women and girls. In this case, the veil serves to distinguish married noble women.

The ladies of the Genoan elite, according to Antonia de Beatis, companion of Cardinal Louis of Aragon during his travels in Italy in 1517, wore a black veil made of taffeta over their shoulders. This was the "mezzaro", which was different than the veils worn in other Italian cities. Vecellio, on the other hand, believes he discovered veiling practices among women belonging to other social groups. According to him, this form of veil was worn as a result of Spanish influence.[62] Veiling practices were part of the fashion in Italian cities such as Genoa, Venice, Padua, and Milan and were generally used to distinguish married women of noble blood.

The veil as fashion accessory formed part of the urban discourses on social difference and identity, much as was the case in Islamic societies. The frequent appearance of veils in Italian cities could also explain why so little attention was

---

60 Bruyns work is different in that it addresses Northeastern Europe (Prussia, Poland, Lithuania, etc.) in detail and thus has a different geographic emphasis.
61 Grassi informs in particular about other cultures.
62 Leyla Belkaid Neri: Croisements et hybridations des modes vestimentaires. In: Isabelle Paresys (ed.): Paraître et apparences en Europe occidentale du Moyen Age à nos jours. Villeneuve d'Ascq, Presses universitaires de Septentrion 2008, pp. 227-242, here p. 230. According to her, the Genoan veil developed from an earlier Antique model that had acquired new meaning through the influence of another veil in the Southern Mediterrannean area. The conjecture that North African influences were at work is unlikely in spite of Genoa's intense trade relationship with Northern Africa (Algeria). The veil's principle function was social differentiation.

given to veiling practices outside of Europe at the time; they were also part of European sartorial practice.

Nature as Distance—Distance as Nature

According to Abraham de Bruyn, there are as many ways to dress oneself as there are differences between the different nations.[63] This statement, however, was based less on empirical knowledge than it was on a peculiar mixture of folklore, new experiences, and images from other media of his time, including speculation.

This combined, piece-meal knowledge was transformed into a cultural cosmological order based on Western Christian values. Distance, according to this world-view, always has both a geographical and a cultural dimension. The further the region was, from a European point of view, the nearer the people living there stood in relation to nature. It was believed that these people wore pelts and that their local heritage was derived from geographic conditions. They appear with names like "the Arabs of the desert", "Arabs of the mountains", or simply "black-skinned Moors." Much like the men, the half-naked females are also considered half-wild and undesirable as sexual partners and wives; they were denied all form of social respect.

Western European identity is, in this case, defined not only through cultural and vestimentary differences with the Other but also through proximity of persons to the centre or the periphery. The centre served as the ego of the author and explains the "apparently" arbitrary treatment of space in the European region.[64]

About fifty years have elapsed at this point in our analysis since Weiditz produced detailed and exact ethnographic portrayals. Since that time, the empirical and ethnological gaze has transformed increasingly into a mechanism of moral judgement that has developed using new criteria for evaluating and creating a hierarchy out of cultures based on clothing, bodies, and gender. The first temporally stable Western European methods of cultural identification were becoming recognizable: nakedness, long hair, adornment, bodily gestures, and poses now differentiated between and created a hierachry of Europeans and Others. Distance and proximity were understood as cultural achievements that determined the level of a society's "civilization."

---

63 „Ut igitur in nationibus magnae dissimilitudines sunt, sic in vestibus existunt etiam maximae varietas." Bruyn, Abraham de: Omnium pene Europae, Asiae, Aphricae Atque Americae Gentium Habitus. Ausgef. von Michiel Colyn, Antwerp 1581, Text II, Vol.

64 Margit Pernau (2008): Bürger mit Turban. Muslime in Delhi im 19. Jahrhundert. Göttingen 2008, p. 14.

Clothing as Epistemic Object

In her comprehensive study, Ulinka Rublack emphasizes the great significance of clothing in the culture of the European Renaissance.[65] The costume books testify to the extent to which visions of the world were structured by clothing cultures. The design and structure of the images is significant because there is usually a large amount of empty space surrounding the clothing illustrations; this empty space fixes the gaze on the clothing. This narrow focus on the clothing as central object constitutes a hiatus with traditional methods of description; as late as the end of the 15th century, travel books recommended beginning with descriptions of cities and their surroundings and then paying attention to the "vulgi moris," that is to say food and clothing.[66] In the costume books, however, clothing is the most important. It appears against a mostly empty or only sparsely adorned space. Daniel Defert has found a compelling explanation for this: the almost empty, white space of the image and the clothing acquire an epistemic status because they replace the mnemonic, filled image space.

The books also refer to the extent to which discovery began to establish itself as a new form of knowledge. With the new relationship of the image to the text, the regime of similarities also changed: it placed experience and portrayal on the same level and gave the image new autonomy.[67] In this manner, the clothed body became the location of the images and a categorical instrument to be used during the experience, discovery, and acquisition of the world. That is why the costume books can be understood as early precursors to an incipient orientalist discourse. In the end, they laid the first foundation stones of an aesthetic hegemony of the West: to be fashionable depended on how one participated in and represented the (European) world.

Translated from German by Claire Wenngren.

---

65 Rublack op. cit.
66 Büttner, op. cit, p. 102.
67 This interpretation as an epistemic location comes from Daniel Defert: Les collections iconographiques du XVIème siècle. In Jean Ceard / Claude Margolin (eds.): Voyager à la Renaissance. Actes du Colloque de Tours 1983. Paris, Maisonneuve et Larose 1987, pp. 531-546, here p. 535-536.

Fig. 1: Christoph Weiditz. Trachtenbuch. 1530/1540, S. 100. Costume of the Moricos Women- and children. Courtesy Germanisches Nationalmuseum Nuremberg.

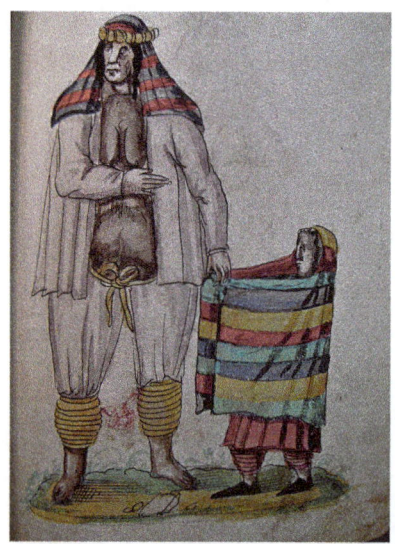

Fig. 2: Sigmundt Heldt. Abconterfaitting allerley Ordenspersonen. „Also gehen die Möriskschen Frauen..." (so go the Morisco women) Courtesy Staatliche Museen zu Berlin, Kunstbibliothek, Lipperheidesche Kostümbibliothek

Fig. 3: Abraham de Bruyn. Omnie poene gentium imagines. (North Africa)
Courtesy Staatliche Museen zu Berlin, Kunstbibliothek, Lipperheidesche Kostümbibliothek

Fig. 4: Jean-Jacques Boissard. Habitus variarum orbis gentium. 1581, p. 61. Femina India Orientalis. Courtesy Staatliche Museen zu Berlin, Kunstbibliothek, Lipperheidesche Kostümbibliothek

Orientalism in 18th and 19th Century Fashion Magazines

Gertrud Lehnert

The way French and German fashion magazines of the 18th and 19th centuries deal with „oriental" aspects of fashionable clothing can be regarded as paradigmatic for the creation of „orientalism" in the sense of Edward Said's definition[1]. Although Said's theory has been widely and justly criticized as one-sided, it nonetheless remains an important tool for the analysis of specific cultural phenomena of past centuries, as well as an indispensable starting point for every reflection on processes of the creation of the *other*.

Magazines have been an essential and influential part of the fashion industry or of the fashion system since the 18th century[2]. They represent a one-sided Eurocentric creation of the „Orient" as the desired and fascinating Other which can easily be dominated and incorporated in the materiality of clothes and accessories, artifacts all the more important because they are inherently linked to the human body. Fashion, incorporating the Other in fragmented bits and pieces, not only dominates the Other by fragmenting and thus destroying it, but in turn also creates a fashionable self-image which is, of course, inextricably linked with culture as a whole.

The paper begins with the outline of my basic assumptions about fashion and specifically orientalist fashion. The main part consists of the description and analysis of exemplary magazines. The center of my argument is the 18th century with the *Cabinet des Modes*, the first real fashion magazine ever (1786-1793). In order to see how things developed, I make connections to the 19th century referring to *Le Moniteur de la Mode* and *Berliner Modenspiegel*[3]. In the end, I briefly discuss the role of text and image and their combination: how do they create certain ideas of (oriental) fashions? Are the two media simply blended? Or can they be considered iconotexts, that is, an inextricable mixture of text and image resulting in more than the sum of its parts?

My general interest is in the history of styles and the production and negotiation of aesthetic values which should ideally be analyzed within the

---

1 Said, Edward (1994): Orientalism [1978], New York: Vintage Books.
2 I borrow the sociological, system theoretical terminology. But being no system theoretician, I use „fashion system" in a different, more general way, as a heuristically useful working term meaning a set of institutions creating and distributing fashionable clothes.
3 There are, of course, many more in the 18th and 19th centuries. But for the sake of the argument, I concentrate on these two. For a broader comparison see my article: Lehnert, Gertrud (2011): "Mode und Orientalismus", in: Iwan D'Aprile, Roland Berbig, Helmut Peitsch, Erhard Schütz (Eds.): Berlins 19. Jahrhundert. Ein Metropolen-Kompendium, Berlin: Akademie Verlag, pp. 95-106 also Lehnert, Gertrud (2007): „Mode als Medium des Kulturtransfers im 18. Jahrhundert", in: Margarete Zimmermann, Gesa Stedmann (Eds.): Höfe — Salons — Akademien. Kulturtransfer und Gender im Europa der Frühen Neuzeit, Hildesheim: Olms Verlag, pp. 309-340.

context of cultural and economical history and the history of mentalities and emotions. Thus, my focus is on the interaction between humans and artifacts as well as on connections between cultural and individual practices, and the motives that generate them (status, economic success, narcissism, desire for beauty etc).

Fashion

Fashion is as an important social sign system as well as a pervasive aesthetic practice of many cultures. In the following, I focus on Western fashion as a special segment of what we may call World Fashion[4].

Basically and on quite an abstract level, fashion can be regarded as a dynamic which is characteristic for modern societies[5] or a dispositif à la Foucault. The first French fashion magazine ever, the *Cabinet des modes*, knew that already and presented, from the beginning, fashionable clothing as part of an entire life style:

„La Mode, qui, dans un Royaume où les Arts sont cultivés (!) avec beaucoup de succès, s'empare de tous les Ouvrages, & les asservit à ses loix, donne la forme aux Meubles de nos Appartemens, comme aux Habits qui nous décorent. Elle les corrige lorsqu'ils sont vicieux, les change lorsqu'ils ont vieilli, les embellit lorsqu'ils sont trop simples pour le siècle du luxe, les simplifie lorsque, trop chargés d'ornemens, ils ne montrent que le travail, & par-là devient la mère de l'industrie & l'ame du commerce. Heureux, lorsque le bon goût a présidé à ceux qui règnent actuellement!"[6].

Clothes can thus be regarded as materializations of the dynamic „fashion". The process of attributing aesthetic and emotional values to articles of clothing and thus transforming them into fashion is the work of (1) the fashion system, a variable set of institutions – designers, producers, magazines, advertisement, fashion guilds etc.[7]; (2) the consumers - objects as well as agents of fashion - in their every day practices[8].

---

4 See, e.g., Eicher, Joanne (ed.) (2010):The Berg Encyclopedia of World Dress and Fashion, (10 vols.); or Riello, Giorgio / McNeil, Peter (2010): The Fashion History Reader. Global Perspectives, London; New York: Routledge.
5 Lipovetsky, Gilles (1987): L'empire de l'éphémère. La mode et son destin dans les sociétés modernes, Paris: Gallimard.
6 "Cabinet des Modes", from Nov. 1785 twice a month; here: March 1786, pp. 67/68.
7 Kawamura, Yuniya (2005): Fashion-ology, An Introduction to Fashion Studies, Oxford; New York: Berg; Entwistle, Joanne (2009): The Aesthetic Economy of Fashion. Markets and Values in Clothing and Modeling, Berg.
8 Lehnert, Gertrud (2006): „Die Kunst der Mode —Zur Einführung", in: Gertrud Lehnert (ed.): Die Kunst der Mode, Oldenburg: dbv, pp.10—25; Lehnert, Gertrud (2004): „Wie wir uns aufführen ... Inszenierungsstrategien von Mode", in: Erika Fischer-Lichte, Clemens Risi, Jens Roselt (eds.): Kunst der Aufführung – Aufführung der Kunst, Berlin: Theater der Zeit, pp. 265-271; Entwistle, Joanne (2001): „The Dressed Body", in: Joanne Entwistle, Elizabeth

That humans endow objects with immaterial qualities the pure material can never possess seems to be an anthropological factor[9]. Men have always used objects in order to give structure and meaning to their lives. Over time, however, those things lost their religious value and were secularized. Fashion seems to provide men with a most important class of objects because clothes are directly linked to the body *and* the imagination. Fashion, after all, is essentially a promise: the promise of the *other* (more often than not a well known other): another self, another body. Fashion promises to make dreams and desires come true, vague and ambivalent as they may be – and it does so with extraordinary effect because fashion is also a practice of the body producing movements, attitudes and self images.[10] And sometimes fashionable clothes can even clarify vague desires and dreams by giving them shape – the shape of a garment ...

Strategy / Emergence

Modern fashion can be characterized as a complex interplay of strategies on the one hand and the sudden emerging of new ideas or forms on the *other* – emerging beyond all strategies and therefore unforeseeable[11]. This is where elements other than institutions come into play: namely the consumers' activity. I ascribe a certain agency to the consumers, although they are doubtless easy to manipulate (which is the aim of all fashion industries), and many of them may be fashion victims. But there is a residuum of personal and cultural predilection and of choice that cannot be explained by strategies but rather by vague desires, dreams and atmospheres[12] closely bound to the material artifacts. „Bound"

Wilson (eds.): Body Dressing, New York: Berg, pp. 33-58; Entwistle, Joanne (2003): The Fashioned Body. Fashion, Dress and Modern Social Theory, Cambridge: Polity.

9 See, among others: Böhme, Hartmut (2006): Fetischismus und Kultur. Eine andere Theorie der Moderne, Reinbek: Rowohlts Enzyklopädie; Kohl, Karl-Heinz (2001): Die Macht der Dinge. Geschichte und Theorie sakraler Objekte, München: Beck; Miller, Daniel (2009): Stuff, Cambridge: John Wiley; Miller, Daniel (2008): The Comfort of Things, Cambridge: Polity Press.

10 Mauss, Marcel (1978): „Die Techniken des Körpers", in: Marcel Mauss: Soziologie und Anthropologie, Band II, Frankfurt etc.: Ullstein 1978 [1950], pp. 199-220: Bourdieu, Pierre (1974): Zur Soziologie der symbolischen Formen, Frankfurt/M.: Suhrkamp; Craik, Jennifer (2009): Fashion. The Key Concepts, London; New York: Berg.

11 See, among others, Entwistle, Joanne (2009): The Aesthetic Economy of Fashion. Markets and Values in Clothing and Modeling, Berg. Cf. also Esposito, Elena (2004): Die Verbindlichkeit des Vorübergehenden: Paradoxien der Mode, Frankfurt/M.: Suhrkamp. For Emergence see: Stephan, Achim (1999): Emergenz: Von der Unvorhersehbarkeit zur Selbstorganisation, Dresden: Dresden University Press; Wägenbaur, Thomas (ed.) (2000): Blinde Emergenz, Interdisziplinäre Beiträge zu Fragen kultureller Evolution, Heidelberg: Synchron; an economic perspective on the functioning af markets: Ackermann, Rolf (2005): „Ökonomie, Tausch und die Macht der Geschichte", in: Georg Mein, Franziska Schössel (eds.): Tauschprozesse. Kulturwissenschaftliche Verhandlungen des Ökonomischen, Bielefeld: Transcript, pp. 157-178.

12 See Certeau, Michel de (1988): Kunst des Handelns, Berlin: Merve Verlag.

means: evoked by them as well as attributed to them. In order for us to consider clothes as a representation of fashion, they must have undergone a complex process of creation, definition, attribution, acceptance, involving many creators, producers, distributors, advertisers etc. But it is, after all, the consumers who live with clothes on an everyday basis. They accept certain clothes or styles as fashion and bring them to life by wearing them – that is: by doing something with the artifacts or better yet: by interacting with the artifacts. It is in cultural performances that clothes are transformed into fashion. And cultural performances, as well as cultural processes in general, can never be completely predicted[13]. Considering the surprises consumers sometimes give to modern trend scouts, we must concede that there is sometimes a „je ne sais quoi", something that eludes planning and strategies, running counter to them - and making fashion a personal and collective adventure. Because fashion (clothes) is more than the decipherable social meaning of clothes. Although a sign system, fashion is deeply ambivalent and volatile in meaning and often eludes meaning altogether. But nevertheless we try to decipher it, to give it meaning.

Fashion system

First forms of a European fashion system have existed at least since the 18th century. It is different from the 20th century fashion system described by Yuniya Kawamura who focuses on the „Fédération Française de la Couture du Prêt-à-Porter des Couturieres et des Créateurs de Mode", the successor of the „Chambre Syndicale de la Haute Couture" (Kawamura 2005) - although the fashion systems of the 18th and still more so of the 19th centuries seem to have been as effective as ours within the contemporary society of those periods with their comparatively more restrained access to luxury and fashion. Ina McCabe has shown convincingly that at the beginning of modern fashion, in the 17th century, the absolutist court as well as the merchants set the rules for fashion[14]. In the 18th century, the system was already quite differentiated. Instead of today's défilés presenting the latest fashion to specialized insiders who are supposed to disseminate them, there were receptions at court, balls, visits to the opera house and other social events giving the upper class ladies the opportunity to wear their latest creations. Almanacs and fashion plates and later fashion magazines described what had been seen and approved by them as fashionable and what they then attempted to distribute to a larger public.[15] In other words: a

---

13 As is the case with every performance. No performance can ever be identical to the others, even if they seem to be the same. See Fischer-Lichte, Erika (2012): Performativität. Eine Einführung, Bielefeld: Transcript, pp. 67 f.
14 McCabe, Ina Baghdiantz (2008): Orientalism in Early Modern France. Eurasian Trade, Exoticism, and the Ancien Régime, Oxford; New York: Berg.
15 Cabinet 1. Oct. 1786, p. 176: „Aussi nous nous sommes associés quelqu'un de beaucoup de goût, qui va habituellement dans les promenades, aux spectacles, qui a le tact sûr pour saisir les nouvelles modes, les nouveautés même qui ne font point encore de mode, &

group of specialists (consumers, dressmakers, milliners ...) create clothes or accessories that they and their customers consider fashionable. The customers wear them (fashion as a practice), the magazines review them, describing and judging the items and the ways they are worn. They declare them to be fashion, they *define* fashion which, in this perspective, comes down to a discourse creating an agreement about what is „in" and what is „out". The reading public is supposed to follow that view and adopt the items as fashion. If they do so, a certain style becomes fashion – and will be „out" as soon as a new style is invented and favored by fashionable people, dress makers, magazines, consumers. This is more or less how fashion works today, only on a much larger scale.

Oriental fashions

Fashion as a dynamic is characterized by change and the emergence of novelties. The *Cabinet des modes* puts this as a motto on each title page: „L'ennui nacquit un jour de l'uniformité". In 1789, they compare English fashion to French fashion. English fashions never changes – declares the French magazine – because the English people look for perfection: „pour varier, il faudroit mille essais, les essais ne peuvent pas avoir la perfection, et ils y renoncent." The French, in contrast, would be extremely bored by perfection, so their fashions change all the time ... [16]

Fashion's purpose, excluding economic gain, is to offer new perceptions and to spark fantasies (an esthetic and a psychological argument). I would argue that the desire for alterity drives fashion. Within this conceptual frame, oriental (or exotic) elements served, since the crusades, as a motor of what was to become Western fashion. Oriental luxury goods could easily fill the need for alterity. They were, from the very beginning, seen as luxurious because they were difficult to acquire, expensive and rare[17]. For the European public, they suggested sensuality, luxury, fantasy, passion, and civilization, but also the opposite: wildness and excess. The exotic was feared and desired at the same time; it represented the fantastic *other* par excellence, the object of desire very

---

qui peuvent le devenir, pour les décrire & pour les peindre. Nous nous flattons que jamais il n'aura paru une robe élégante, un habit bien coupé, bien fait, qu'il ne l'ait vu, & ne l'ait annoncé."

16 Cabinet 1789, 1. mars, p. 76.

17 Berg, Maxine / Eger, Elizabeth (eds.) (2008): Luxury in the Eighteenth-Century: Debates, Desires and Delectable Goods, Basingstoke etc.: Palgrave; Riello, Giorgio (ed.) (2009b): How India Clothed the World: The World of South Asian Textiles, 1500-1850, Leiden: Brill (with Tirthankar Roy); Riello, Giorgio / McNeil, Peter (2010): The Fashion History Reader. Global Perspectives, London; New York: Routledge; McCabe, Ina Baghdiantz (2008): Orientalism in Early Modern France. Eurasian Trade, Exoticism, and the Ancien Régime, Oxford, NY: Berg.

far away from contemporary familiar life and yet, quickly incorporated, could become part of the familiar and thus devoid of its menacing aspects.[18]

Ambivalence is deeply ingrained in the Western reception of the exotic. Against all probability, exotic objects have – more or less – retained these attributes, although the knowledge in regards to them has increased: the knowledge about their material side, about the regions they come from, about where and under which circumstances they are produced (and later imitated), but also about their „immaterial" side: how the ideas they embody are constructed as images and clichés in order to serve different power politics. Nevertheless, their "fantastic" side remains. In an individual – psychological – perspective one could call that process repression. We know (intellectually) how things work, bu**t we don't want to. And this is exactly why they can keep their power and become the agent of individual behaviour as well as of cultural processes.

Orientalism in fashion can thus be analyzed as a paradigm of fashion, because it clearly demonstrates how fashion as a concept works, and what role the institutions play in this process. The fashion system disguises its inherent consumerist logic of rejecting the old in order to sell the new products as the promise of the *other* which, of course, can never be fulfilled. The *other* is desired, but never as a whole: new products, like new art, are only accepted by the public when they present a good „mélange" of the well-known with the unknown, of tradition with innovation. Oriental styles, the exotic other par excellence in the 18th and 19th centuries, are therefore never introduced or, for that matter, accepted as a whole, but only in fragments that can easily be appropriated, made part of the „own" while still nourishing the fantasy of being special and exotic[19].

Fashion in Early Magazines

When fashion magazines stepped onto the European stage, oriental luxury goods had long (since the end of the 17th century) become a normal part of the elite life style[20] and were being imitated by French and other manufacturers. As early as the 17th century, French and Dutch manufacturers started to imitate

---

18 In a political context, it could be used for specific purposes, as Ina McCabe has demonstrated.
19 Lehnert, Gertrud (2007): „Mode als Medium des Kulturtransfers im 18. Jahrhunder", in: Margarete Zimmermann, Gesa Stedmann (eds.): Höfe — Salons — Akademien. Kulturtransfer und Gender im Europa der Frühen Neuzeit, Hildesheim: Olms Verlag, pp. 309-340; Lehnert, Gertrud (2010): „Des "robes à la turque" et autres orientalismes à la mode", in: Anja Bandau, Marcel Dorigny, Rebekka von Mallinckrodt (eds.): Les mondes coloniaux à Paris au XVIIIe siècle. Circulation et enchevêtrement des savoirs, Paris: Karthala, pp. 183-200.
20 Baghdiantz McCabe 2008; Berg, Maxine (2005): Luxury and Pleasure in Eighteenth-Century Britain, Oxford: Oxford University Press; Berg/Eger 2008.

patterns and techniques. Cotton, however, was a new invention: „Cotton emerged as a fashionable fabric in the 1780s with the *chemise à la reine*, the cotton shift favored by Marie Antoinette beginning in this turbulent decade. As always, clothing had political and international implications. One of the chief reasons the Lyon silk manufacturers railed against the reductive modern attire is that their luxurious silks were being abandoned in favor of imported cottons from India"[21].

I agree with Ina McCabe's assumption that oriental (sartorial) splendor at the French court of Louis XIV gave rise to the creation of „Frenchness" through fashion[22]. Orientalism did not only change French society, its economy, life styles and self definitions, but also those of many other European (or Western) countries who followed the French example accepting France/Paris as the global „arbiter elegantiarum". A means for being informed were fashion magazines – the French originals, but also the Imitations in other countries like Germany.

But France was not only the subject of transformation, as McCabe writes, but transformed and formed itself under the influence of orientalism, materially and socially. This works because of the intricate interrelation between material culture, economic considerations, status questions, cultural and individual fantasies, desires, and narcissisms.

Like fashion magazines today, the magazines in the 18th and 19th century are life style-magazines.

They consist of different parts: essays on current cultural events (theatre, literature, exhibitions, furniture, architecture, travels etc.) are combined with ideas for interior decorating or fashionable coaches or advice for travel in fashionable places (mostly in France). In the 19th century, there were more and more serialized novels and short stories.

But the heart of it all is, of course, the fashion plates and their descriptions and discussions. The *Cabinet*[23] consisted of about 8 pages of text and 3 fashion plates – quite a good proportion; it first came out fortnightly, later three times per month.[24] Adressing a wealthy bourgeois public, the magazines often suggest

---

21 "Robe à l'anglaise [French] (1991.204a,b)". In Heilbrunn Timeline of Art History. New York: The Metropolitan Museum of Art, 2000: http://www.metmuseum.org/toah/hd/eudr/ho_1991.204a,b.htm (September 2008), 25. Okt. 2009, 10.21 Uhr. See also Riello, Giorgio / Parthasarathi, Prasannan (eds.) (2009): The Spinning World: A Global History of Cotton Textiles, 1200-1850, Oxford: Oxford University Press.

22 McCabe 2008.

23 Ed. François Buisson.

24 Kleinert, Annemarie (1980): Die frühen Modejournale in Frankreich. Studien zur Literatur der Mode von den Anfängen bis 1848, Berlin: Erich Schmidt; Kleinert, Annemarie (1993): „Original oder Kopie? Das Journal des Dames et des Modes (1797—1839) und seine zahlreichen Varianten", in: Deutsches Historisches Institut Paris (ed.): Francia. Forschungen zur westeuropäischen Geschichte, Bd. 20/3, pp. 99—120; Lehnert, Gertrud (2007): „Mode als Medium des Kulturtransfers im 18. Jahrhundert", in: Margarete Zimmermann, Gesa

an elitist character. Readers could find addresses of milliners, dressmakers, modistes and other important fashion information.[25] Almost never to be found are reports on the origin of oriental or exotic goods, or on trade. The luxury goods are presented as coming out of nowhere, which implies that the power relations making them possible are invisible (typical for the distribution of fashion in general). Sometimes, however, there are allusions, so e.g. when, following the theories of the day, the *Cabinet* explains that different climates in different regions of the World produce different ethnic characters[26].

Aspects of the orient

What does „oriental" mean in the 18th century? More or less everything east of Western Europe, including Greece, Russia, India, Persia, declares Diderot's *Encyclopédie*[27].

What do the magazines tell their readers about the Orient or, more specifically, about oriental clothing? In the second cahier, the *Cabinet* lets us know that in the Orient, men wear „de longs vêtemens, qui ont de l'ampleur & de la noblesse"; and the same is true for colder climates like in Russia or Poland: they sometimes did spread a „luxe oriental". It comes as no surprise that keywords are: luxe, ampleur, noblesse.

In wet climates however, men wear narrow trousers in order to protect themselves from dirt. Women, in contrast, seem to behave quite differently, not at all considering practical questions:

„mais les femmes sont au-dessus des inconvéniens du climat & de l'intempérie des saisons. Les Françoises, principalement dans la Capitale, qui est le centre du goût, savent imiter & s'approprier même les Costumes de toutes les

---

Stedmann (eds.): Höfe — Salons — Akademien. Kulturtransfer und Gender im Europa der Frühen Neuzeit, Hildesheim: Olms Verlag, pp. 309-340; Lehnert, Gertrud (2011): „Mode und Orientalismus", in: Roland Berbig, Iwan D'Aprile, Helmut Peitsch, Erhard Schütz (eds.): Berlins 19. Jahrhundert. Ein Metropolen-Kompendium. Berlin: Akademie Verlag, pp. 95-106; Zika, Anna (2006): Ist alles eitel? Zur Kulturgeschichte deutschsprachiger Modejournale zwischen Aufklärung und Zerstreuung, 1750—1950, Weimar: VDG; Ackermann, Astrid (2005): Paris, London und die europäische Provinz: die frühen Modejournale 1770—1830, Frankfurt/M. u.a.: Lang; Kuhles, Doris (2000): „Das ‚Journal des Luxus und der Moden' (1786—1827). Zur Entstehung seines inhaltlichen Profils und seiner journalistischen Struktur", in: Gerhard R. Kaiser (ed.): Friedrich Justin Bertuch (1747—1822). Verleger, Schriftsteller und Unternehmer im klassischen Weimar, Tübingen: Niemeyer, pp. 489—500.

25 Even the German magazines starting with the Journal des Luxus und der Moden, 1786ff. give adresses of French dressmakers, coiffeurs etc.

26 Cabinet 1787, cahier 23, pp. 3-7. - Cahier 22: pp. 14-16; Idées diverses sur la beauté.

27 Diderot, Denis / d'Alembert, Jean Le Rond (eds.): Encyclopédie, ou dictionnaire raisonné des sciences, des arts et des métiers, 1751-1772,. For a thourough investagation of the contemporary knowledge about the Orient, about myths and realities, trade and travels, see Osterhammel, Jürgen (1998): Die Entzauberung Asiens. Europa und die asiatischen Reiche im 18. Jahrhundert, München: Beck.

Nations. Aux robbes *Françoises* elles ont fait succéder les *Polonoises*, aux Polonoises les *Lévites*, aux *Lévites* les robbes à *l'Angloise* & à la *Turque*. Dans cette dernière, une jolie femme, soit au Spectacle, ou dans un Cercle, remporte des triomphes plus sûrs & plus agréables que ceux d'une Géorgienne ou Circassienne dans les Harems de Constantinople. Il n'est pas même de Sultane qui ne fût jalouse de son élégance, de sa grace, & des hommages qu'on lui rend."[28]

Western superiority goes without saying in the *Cabinet's* perspective. A French woman in an orientalizing garb (having appropriated and mixed it with the contemporary European style) will always be more beautiful, more graceful, more s*eductive than any Oriental woman.

In the articles, it becomes obvious that it is often just the dress' name alluding to the Orient. A „robe à la turque" is not really inspired by turkish fashions (whatever they may have been in Turkish or European eyes). It is simply the name that suggests oriental luxury, as do the „robes à la Sultane" or the „robes aux Lévites". Even important may be that the orientalizing names classify, specify and differentiate internal aspects of Parisian fashion, like cuts and styles of drapery. That means, they remain completely within the system of European fashion[29].

By doing so, they are indicative of the Western attitude towards the *other*: it is used as an alluring yet exploitable discoursive element for the self-construction, just as Edward Said analyzed European Literature in the age of Imperialism. On the other hand, oriental goods had long been produced in Asia for the European market taking into account Western tastes and fashions. Thus, in a certain sense the *Other* as an active partner of its own marketing, but certainly in a dubious role since those who really produced the items were in no way involved in mechanisms of trade, image-building and so on.

The parallels to today's fashion system are evident. Clothes are produced in low-wage countries mainly in Asia; so are „Asian" products for the Western markets. The exploitation of workers is known yet deliberately ignored by consumers; it becomes part of the adoption and incorporation of fashion in the West. Or, for that matter, in the world. And styles, once Asian or other, have become a differentiating aspect of Western design.

By the end of the 18th century, the most fashionable imports from India were cashmere shawls, soon imitated in Scotland (Paisley) and elsewhere in Europe.

---

28 15. 1. 1786, p. 34.
29 Cabinet des Modes, 24ième Cahier, 1er Novembre 1786, Planche I: „A la Toussaint l'on prend tous les habits d'hiver (...) & le satin sera l'habit des femmes , comme il l'est depuis un tems immémorial. (...) Robe à la Turque; elle est d'un satin à aies violettes & vertesLes manches & le corset de dessous la robe, sont d'un satin couleur queue de serin. (...) Bonnet à la Turque ...gaze anglaise, plumes,

French writers never tire of declaring that only women from Paris, the capital of fashion, possess true elegance. Or, as we can read in *Le Moniteur de la Mode* six decades later:

„L'Inde nous enverra toujours ses riches cachemires, l'Angleterre et la Belgique leurs féeriques dentelles, la Russie et le Brésil leurs pierreries étincelantes, mais les Parisiennes seules diront le secret de les porter, de les chiffoner et d'en faire des bijoux admirables."[30]

Edward Said's (Said 1994) analysis of the Orient as a construction of the West, aiming at forging the West's proper identity via the Oriental Other, could find no better proof than that. The West declares itself implicitly in possession of power, including the power of aesthetic judgement which, in turn, includes the implicit judgement of the state of civilization as a whole. The Parisians may not be able to produce the beautiful fabrics, but they alone can make them elegant – and, in a way, make sense of them.

In the 19th century, styles of dresses were no longer named as they were in the 18th century. Their description in fashion magazines usually included the exact information about the fabric. Oriental aspects are only to be found in the verbal description. They are, however, an integral part of the ensemble and rarely marked as special. Beautiful and tasteful, the fabric implicitly suggests a desirable feeling of sensuality and luxury; they contribute to fashion's ever-ambivalent promise without ever making it too special.

The description of the engraving goes as follows (p. 99):

„Costume de cachemire de l'inde bleu douanier et broché turc, pour une fille des seize ans. – Jupe de cachemire garni de deux plissés. Sur le devant est posé un tablier de cachemire bouillonné et coulissé, terminé par une draperie de broche. – Deux lés de cachemire encadrent le tablier; ils sont arrondis et se drapent sur les cotés. Dans le dos tombe un lé relevé en plis de burnous et bordé d'une liséré de broché. (...)

Performativity

I would like to briefly turn to the modern implications of the statement that „les Parisiennes seules diront le secret de les porter, de les chiffoner et d'en faire des bijoux admirables." This reads like a theoretical stance known today as „performativity"; it reads like an early statement on the performativity of fashion.

Clothes have to be worn to become elegant, graceful and *really* attractive – in other words: to become fashion. Implied is the incorporation, and thus a power relation. Dress and person become one, at least for a moment, and so the oriental aspects are no longer the *Other*, but the self.

---

30 Moniteur de la Mode, June 2nd 1848, p. 38.

If clothes have to be worn in order to become graceful, they perform the reverse function simultaneously: adorn women and make them more attractive. In a letter to the editor (whether fake or authentic is unclear) a (provincial) woman writes that she won her future husband's heart thanks to the beautiful „robe à la Turque" and her „chapeau à la Captif", even though he, at the time, was also attracted to another woman.

Il „balançoit encore entre l'or de ma Rivale et mes foibles appas; mais aidée de ce galant costume, j'achevai de le vaincre & de le décider en ma faveur. (...) je dois cette victoire, Messieurs, à votre charmant *Cabinet*".[31] She begs the editor to continue giving detailed information on fashion because she wants to keep her husband by being every day „new" („Et quel moyen plus sûr que celui de paroître tous les jours nouvelle à ses yeux, en variant mes ajustemens?").

Fashion is considered as a means to be sexually attractive, to play the part in the heterosexual dance[32]. It is no coincidence that the woman pretends to think that a dress alluding to the orient helped her to be more seductive than her rival. As I said, a *robe à la Turque* does not really possess oriental characteristics in style or cut. But the dress' name alone suffices to set off a set of ideas and fantasies – like the desire of being sexually attractive as oriental women in the harem were believed to be. The idea to become more attractive in a certain garb will help everyone to feel more attractive and behave more like an attractive person – another aspect of performativity, more in the sense of John Austin's philosophy of language, *How to do Things with Words* (1962).

I would like to argue that the image of the sexually seductive woman put forth in that letter serves as an antidote to the *Cabinet's* observation that women imitate more and more often male fashion – something the *Cabinet* judges with ambivalence. Thus, ideas of female subservience, sensuality and eroticism might be used to balance the new and not so welcome development that women, emancipated, might start to compete with men.

Imitation

Another key word in the text of the *Cabinet* is imitation; the Parisian women „savent *imiter*". Imitation is at the center of orientalism as it is at the very heart of fashion. Fashion consists partially of the imitation of others. „Imitation" includes concepts as diverse as emulation, dependence, competition, appropriation, incorporation and dominance. In the best case a lady is able to give an individual twist to the imitation, a precise embodiment of her personal way of wearing clothes and accessories. Thus it is a manner, an attitude which

---

31 Cabinet, February 2nd 1786, p. 61.
32 Hollander, Anne (1993): Seeing Through Clothes, Berkeley; Los Angeles; London; Lehnert, Gertrud (2010): "Gender", in: Berg Encyclopedia of World Dress and Fashion, vol. 8: West Europe, Oxford: Berg, pp. 452-461.

makes the difference. Fashion's paradox, as Elena Esposito[33] puts it as well as Georg Simmel, Christian Garve and many others have done since the 18th century, is that while wishing to discern oneself as special and individualistic, everybody wears what everybody else wears.

The *Berliner Modenspiegel* declared in 1832 that Berlin is less dictatoral in fashion than Paris, less innovative than London, but it „ist doch bekannt dafür, dass es nicht nur die fremden Produkte alle führt, sondern auch nachahmt, auf eine Weise, dass seine Nachahmungen an Güte, Dauer und Billigkeit die ursprünglichen Produkte bei Weitem übertreffen." [34] Imitation is nothing to be ashamed of, on the contrary: imitation as a means to enrich the proper culture is judged to be absolutely necessary and even admirable.

Fashionable vocabulary

I already mentioned the „robes à la Turque", „à la Sultane" etc. Coats are made of „drap d'orient" or „gros des Indes", others have turkish patterns, „négligés" have pagoda sleeves; Parisian ladies wear „turbans of the latest taste" (*Berliner Modenspiegel*, Heft 7, 1832), etc. Often there is not even a material oriental element in the clothes but it is simply the name given to a certain style that suggests „Orient": robe à la Turque, à la Polonaise, à la Circassienne etc.[35]

The arbitrariness of naming is also present in the following remark referring to very slight modifications of accessories or dresses that do not really alter the dress but pretend to do so by giving it a new name: „les noms différens que l'on donne aux robes, ne veulent pas dire que leur forme soit différente."[36]

Obviously, the words used to describe a certain style (*robe à la Turque*), tissu or pattern are already well known at the time because no fashion magazine ever explains them. German magazines don't even translate them into German: the fashion terminology is beyond any doubt French, as French fashion sets the rules and is presented as the only one worthy of imitation (except for some English exceptions).

Heterogeneity

The indecision as to which countries belong to the fashionable Orient is mirrored in the heterogeneity of the clothes. Not only is a „robe à la Turque" made of „taffetas des Indes gris de perles" (the words alone sound poetic ...), but

---

33 Esposito, Elena (2004): Die Verbindlichkeit des Vorübergehenden: Paradoxien der Mode. Frankfurt/M.: Suhrkamp.
34 „Berliner Modenspiegel. Eine Zeitschrift für die elegante Welt", redigiert von W.v.Kesteloott, ab 7. Januar 1832, hier: am 22. Juni 1832 (22. Nummer), vorgeschalteter Werbeeinleger.
35 Cf. Cabinet 1787, cahier 6, p. 314.
36 Cabinet 1789, January 1st, p. 28.

the magazines never offer a complete oriental costume or a complete and homogeneous style - except in masquerades.

The incorporation of „oriental" elements never results in a homogenous „oriental" image. Un „pouf à la chinoise" ressembles a „bonnet à la Turque"[37], a small turban-like hat is worn with a Biedermeier-ball gown. Widespread is the combination of a Western silhouette with an oriental pattern:

„Russian, German, and French Rococo styles absorbed chinoiserie into a seamless whole of *frivoles, fêtes galantes*, and colorful narratives. One particular syncretism is evident in painted wallpapers and dress, where the traditional Western floral forms in Rococo taste cross-pollinated with meandering Chinese patterns."[38]

„Oriental" means a patchwork, consisting of fragments of diverse origin, dominated by contemporary Western styles mixed with some foreign (or foreign-sounding) elements. On a more formal level, this process can also be explained by the necessity to find a balance between old and new. Formalist literary theory holds that literature (or art or fashion, for that matter), in order to be labeled high-quality, should never completely satisfy the audience's expectations (the result would be banal or „kitsch"), but needs to present enough innovation in order to disturb the audience's expectations („Erwartungshorizont" in the terminology of reception theory/Rezeptionsästhetik) and change it. Too much innovation, however, would have the opposite effect: It would not be understood, it would be irritating and thus be rejected. The secret is the right measure of mixing old and new, known and unknown.

This model can be transferred to fashion which also needs the right balance of tradition and innovation. A complete Indian, Chinese or Turkish Outfit would have destroyed the idea of fashion (as a Western concept). It would have been perceived as masquerade („ethno-masquerade" as Kader Konuk[39] puts it, talking about Lady Mary Wortley Montagu's efforts to partly assimilate Turkish dress while in Istanbul). The wearer would have felt estranged from her context and her culture's ideas of elegance, which for Europeans long remained invariably linked to Western ideas[40].

Fragmentation of strange, „exotic" styles and the subsequent incorporation of fragments into familiar fashion results in an alluring whole containing enough strange elements to arouse curiosity and the experience of something „new",

---

37 Cabinet 1786, November 1st., 7.
38 "Dresses (robe a la polonaise) (1976.146a,b_1970.87)", in: Heilbrunn Timeline of Art History. New York: The Metropolitan Museum of Art, 2000: http://www.metmuseum.org/toah/hd/orie/ho_1976.146a,b_1970.87.htm (October 2006) (25. October 2009, 9.30 a.m.).
39 Konuk, Kader (2004): „Ethnomasquerade in Ottoman-European Encounters: Reenacting Lady Mary Wortley Montagu", in: Criticism 46.3 (2004), pp. 393-414.
40 As mentioned in the Introduction, the history of fashion has begun to be written in a global perspective, see, e.g., Riello, Giorgio / McNeil, Peter (eds.) (2010): The Fashion History Reader. Global Perspectives, London; New York: Routledge.

while familiar elements allow the wearer to feel safe. „Incorporation" is a key word to describe this process of taking possession. Closely tied to the body, fashion is pivotal in the neverending story of self-fashioning. As a body practice[41], it can easily incorporate the „exotic" and thus make it a part of the familiar. Thus, control and a clear power hierarchy is established in the process of adapting a new fashion, all the more so if the new elements are „oriental" ones.[42]

Text/Illustration or Word and Image

Like fashion magazines today, the magazines in the 18th and 19th century are lifestyle magazines. They offer essays on current cultural events (theatre, literature, exhibitions, furniture, architecture, travel, etc.), ideas for interior decoration, presentations of coaches or chinaware, even ideas for trips to fashionable places (mostly in France). Anecdotes, serialized novels and short stories entertain the reader. But at the heart of them all is fashion, the written descriptions of clothes often accompanied by fashion plates (just three in the early *Cabinet*).

Among the key words are: beautiful, special, gracious. They imply aesthetic judgements meant as a general, undebatable norm. This conforms with the 18th century conviction that beauty was a definable characteristic of things. Although addressing a larger public than fashion news ever had before, the magazines are eager to suggest an elitist character (and since they were expensive and printed in small numbers, they were). Ever more frequently, addresses of milliners, dressmakers, modistes and other merchants of fashionable items are advertised, be it in the form of articles on certain accessories including the address where they can be bought, or manifesting in advertisements. Even the German magazines starting with the *Journal des Luxus und der Moden*, (786ff) give addresses of *French* dressmakers, coiffeurs etc. Rarely found are reports on the origin of oriental or exotic goods, or on trade.

Due to technical complexities there are few illustrations in the early fashion magazines. Thus, the exclusivity of visual representation is underlined. The texts, in contrast, carry the main burden of suggesting mental images of the current fashions. The comprehensive and precise descriptions of clothes, accessories, how to wear them as well as the occasion and the place where they

---

41 Mauss, Marcel (1978): "Die Techniken des Körpers", in: Marcel Mauss: Soziologie und Anthropologie Bd II, Frankfurt etc.: Ullstein [1950], pp. 199-220; Craik, Jennifer (2009): Fashion. The Key Concepts, London; New York: Berg; Entwistle, Joanne / Wilson, Elizabeth (eds.) (2001): Body Dressing, London; New York: Berg; Entwistle, Joanne (2000): The Fashioned Body. Fashion, Dress and Modern Society, London; New York: Berg.

42 Although the process is in some sense double-sided. European/Western styles have been adopted in Asia and oriental consumer goods have been produced according to Western tastes fort he Western markets.

should be worn, make fashionable items recognizable. The illustrations are also very informative, they show the clothes in detail in order to make them imitable.

The textual parts that have nothing to do with wardrobe set the tone for the reception of clothes, especially stories and the anecdotes. In our present context, those containing an „oriental" aspect are worth noting because they sometimes create powerful images that underline the message of clothes, accessories and furniture. In one anecdote (*Cabinet* 1786, cahier 3, p. 15), for example, an unfaithful „oriental" wife declares that she conceived her new born illegitimate baby via snow from the prophet (a clear allusion to the Western myth of Jupiter's masquerades as a golden rain). Her husband sells the child into slavery and tells the wife that her son melted. The anecdote, obviously fabricated by a European, suggests that oriental women are mendacious, sensual, and unfaithful. Oriental men complement their shortcomings with cleverness, ruthlessness and dishonesty.

Almost 100 years later, the *Berliner Modenspiegel*[43] offers a novel in sequels about a young Danish man going to India, falling in love with a beautiful Indian girl with the very un-indian name Agathe. He marries her against her father's will – and regrets the marriage for the rest of his life. Agathe is selfish, mean, fickle, unfaithful. She has love affairs, and finally leaves her husband and children in order to lead a life of dissolution (instead of conforming to the 19th century bourgois ideal of a wife dedicating her life to husband and children). The consequences are fatal for the entire family: Bernhard loses his children and dies a miserable death.

These are negative variations of the fantasy of the sensuous, erotically liberated, civilised harem beauty which had had so much impact on the European imagination since at least the 17th century, variations of the fantasy of the oriental femme fatale, sexually insatiable and destroyer of men, so popular in the late 19th century. *Berliner Modenspiegel* No 11 gives the account of someone visiting a woman in childbed in Damaskus, calling up the Western fantasies of the luxurious harem closed from the world. Walking through ugly, dirty streets and a bazaar, the Western visitor perceives luxury goods which have been produced in England (!). When he finally reaches and enters the house he is struck by its interior of splendid luxury and the most beautiful women gathered around the equally beautiful lady in childbed ... The narrator gives the cynical advice that it would be better to send merchants instead of missionaries into the colonized countries. Cultural transfer via trade – quite an old concept, if not completely outdated in the middle of the 19th century (having already been practiced for centuries).[44]

---

43 Berliner Modenspiegel, 1848 (ab Heft 12), author: Gräfin von W. (?), title: „Bernhard und Agathe, Oder die Fahrt nach Ostindien"
44 Cf. Berg, Maxine / Eger, Elizabeth (eds.) (2008): Luxury in the Eighteenth-Century: Debates, Desires and Delectable Goods, Basingstoke, etc.: Palgrave; Baghdiantz McCabe, Ina

As in modern fashion magazines, stories and anecdotes are part of advertising strategies in fashion by setting a tone, suggesting a mood. Oriental fashions are thus implicitly marked as alluring and at the same time dangerous, even despicable. It is the schizophrenic strategy of power relations to warn people against the ugliness and meanness of the pretended „reality" of the Orient, while at the same time advertising oriental styles, tissus and accessories. But these have, obviously, long since become part of European fashion, thus become „civilized", and are no longer perceived as „truly" oriental (implying: untamed). What they still possess is what I would call their fantastic quality: they are forever marked by an atmosphere of the unknown, of beauty, luxury and sensuality.

Not only texts, but also illustrations can become mediums for telling stories and creating atmospheres. In the *Magasin des Modes Nouvelles, françaises et anglaises* (the new name of the *Cabinet des modes*) readers are informed on December 10, 1787, that the three illustrations that had been published each on its own page, should be assembled on one larger, folding page thus allowing one to create dramatic scenes:

„de ces actions que l'on voit tous les jours dans la société, de ces scènes qui attachent sans effrayer, des scènes comiques, en un mot, qui sont dans la nature , & non des scènes tragiques, qui sont toujours hors nature, ou dans les convulsions extraordinaires de la nature." (17/18)

The argument closely follows the theatre aesthetics of the time. But in contrast to the texts, the illustrations are in need of an interpretation because they cannot make their message perfectly clear[45]. The first illustration shows a young man and two women. The text interprets it as follows: a young man leaves his beloved because he loves another lady, who, in turn, leaves without pausing to listen to him. The first lady is desperate and hopeless. But the commentator himself warns his readers against an unambiguous interpretation in concluding that the illustration is harmless enough and open for many interpretations: they should make their own interpretattion. Despite the

---

(2008): Orientalism in Early Modern France. Eurasian Trade, Exoticism, and the Ancien Régime, Oxford: Berg; Berg, Maxine (2005): Luxury and Pleasure in Eighteenth-Century Britain, Oxford: Oxford University Press; Bayerdörfer, Hans-Peter; Eckhart Hellmuth (eds.) (2003): Exotica. Konsum und Inszenierung des Fremden im 19. Jahrhundert, Münster: LIT Verlag; Wolter, Stefanie (2005): Die Vermarktung des Fremden. Exotismus und die Anfänge des Massenkonsums, Frankfurt/M.; New York: Campus Verlag . For cultural transfer via fashion see: Lehnert, Gertrud (2007): „Mode als Medium des Kulturtransfers im 18. Jahrhundert", in: Margarete Zimmermann, Gesa Stedmann (eds.): Höfe — Salons — Akademien. Kulturtransfer und Gender im Europa der Frühen Neuzeit, Hildesheim: Olms Verlag, pp. 309-340.

45 In Renaissance costume books, it is the other way round – see Gabriele Mentges' text in this book.

promising declaration that images, too, tell stories, the same openness and ambivalence characterizes all other illustrations in the early magazines.

The commentary of the négligé goes as follows:
„Il est impossible que cette mode ne soit encore due aux Ambassadeurs Indiens. Assurément, ce seront les Marchandes de robes qui auront plus conçu de modes à l'Indienne, & qui auront imaginé les modes les plus agréables."
Beyond the somewhat sobre commentary, I can hardly imagine a story woven into the illustration: it does not really possess a narrative substrate, and its purpose is simply to show clothes in a comprehensive and alluring way and make them ripe for imitation. They concentrate on that which seemed indispensable for contemporary fashion information: the outfits, worn by ladies and gentlemen moving in a way that clearly showed the garments. The text indicates the style's pretended origins from India, according to popular imagination a land of wealth and sumptuousness, and contrasts this to the merchants making and selling the clothes in Paris – so it alludes at least to the two aspects of oriental clothing: their origin and their trade.

Although illustrations and texts are separated, even by pages, they relate to each other, but in a rather loose way. The two media do not form a new entity coming close to what we call today „iconotext", the unseparable entity of both media[46].

By the 19th century, this had radically changed. Fashion illustrations were now very often full-blown pictures of family or social scenes (see illustrations 2, 3 and 4).

However, there still is no close connection between image and text. The image is trusted to tell its own fashion-story and communicate its message through direct visual effects. It also offers more and more explicit visual contexts in which the clothes should or coud be worn because a fashionable lady at the times changed her outfit several times a day and needed to know what to wear for which occassion – and occasions are always bound to certain places. The modern principle of telling visual or textual stories in order to situate clothes in a (not too specific) context is paramount in the magazines as the adequate way to interest readers and give the clothes a history. And it is clear that visual stories should never be too precise in order to leave a reader free to read the story in the way most appealing to her.

---

46 Wagner, Peter (1996): "Introduction: Ekphrasis, Iconotexts, and Intermediality – the State(s) of the Art(s)", in: Peter Wagner (ed.): Icons - Texts - Iconotext. Essays on Ekphrasis and Intermediality. Berlin, New York: de Gruyter-Verlag, pp. 1-40;. Möllendorff, Peter von: Ikonotexte – Versuch eines multiperspektivischen Zugangs (http://fss.plone.uni-giessen.de/fss/fbz/fb04/institute/altertum/philologie/dokumentationen/ikonotexte-duale-mediensituationen/resume/file/resume.pdf)

Incarnations of Alterity: Orient or History

The desire for the *other* is manifest in a predilection for the exotic, but also in a predilection for history as quite another form of alterity. Clothes can serve as a means of personal and cultural memory – as is recycling styles, forms, functions. And still another one are clothes named after important events like the king's vaccination, a ship wreck or the history of a woman injustly condemned to be burned at the stake („caraco à l'Inconnue reconnue ou à la cauchoise"[47]).

If this is true for the late 18th century, it is all the more so, of course, for the 19th century. When it comes to forms and styles, I do not really perceive a difference between the enthusiasm for styles à la Gabrielle d'Estrées, Mary Stuart, Clarissa Harlowe (!) or else medieval ones, and those for styles à l'indienne, à la grecque, circassienne etc. It is only the fabrics that make the difference. There are no historical fabrics, but there are „oriental" ones: and they have already in the 18th century become normal, although they are still marked – more or less implicitly – as special.

Madeleine Delpierre argues that the oriental influence prepared the softer style of the empire-fashion[48], et Koda/Martin write: „The vista of the East has altered Western life and dress", that is: material as well as formes and styles[49].

Fashion, I would conclude, never respects the Other as other, in its peculiarity. It serves as a reservoir of visual forms, of vague connotations and fantasies, of sensuous appeals[50]. But as such, oriental elements serve as a motor for the self-definition of the West and, more specifically, of Western fashion just because – as the exotic, the *Other* par excellence - they seem to invite allow for creative interpretations, the making of a choice, a strategy. However, in analogy to the fate of artistic avantgardes, the new stimuli in fashion are quickly incorporated into the mainstream and become „normal" and thus harmless.51 Oriental elements, however, retain some of their „exotic" appeal. Even though they may become familiarized, their „exotic" appeal can easily be revitalized and re-marked as „new".

---

47 Cabinet, October 1st. 1786, pp.169ff

48 Delpierre, Madeleine (1997): Dress in France in the 18th Century, New Haven: Yale University Press; p. 68; Ribeiro, Aileen (2002?): Dress in Eighteenth-Century Europe, New Haven; London: Yale University Press.

49 Koda, Harold / Martin, Richard (1994): Orientalism. Visions of the East in Western Dress, New York: The Metropolitan Museum of Art.

50 Brand, Jan / Teunissen, José (eds.) (2005): Global Fashion - Local Tradition. On the Globalization of Fashion, Arnhem: Terra; reviewed by Lehnert, Gertrud (2010): „Karneval der Stile / Über "Global Fashion - Local Tradition. On the Globalization of Fashion", in: Texte zur Kunst 78, Juni 2010, pp. 162-165.

51 See, amoung others, Narumi, Hiroshi (2000): "Fashion Orientalism and the Limits of Counter Culture", in: Postcolonial Studies 3.3. (2000), p. 311-29.

In a new context, they work as familiar elements albeit possessing enough appeal to be, time and again, marked as special, new, interesting, beautiful, sometimes even enigmatic. The fragments Western fashions incorporate from Oriental clothing need not be situated in a specific geographical, political, cultural space.
Their origin is of no interest, except in rare cases when a shawl is marked as an authentic one because it really comes from India. As fashionable elements among many others, they can be imitated, incorporated and used like the others. They are subject to the same revaluations and devaluations and are, as exotic elements, hardly more interesting than – let's say: historical novelties.

Ill. 1 : Cabinet des modes, 15 january 1786: Femme en robbe à la Turque (Courtesy Staatliche Museen zu Berlin, Kunstbibliothek, Sammlung Modebild – Lipperheidesche Kostümbibliothek)

Illustr. 2: Journal des Dames et des Modes, 1847, Tome 98, vol. 2, p 255 (Courtesy Staatliche Museen zu Berlin, Kunstbibliothek, Sammlung Modebild – Lipperheidesche Kostümbibliothek)

Illustr. 3: Moniteur de la Mode 1880, 28. Februar, gravure 1687 (Courtesy Staatliche Museen zu Berlin, Kunstbibliothek, Sammlung Modebild – Lipperheidesche Kostümbibliothek)

Illustr. 4: *Cabinet des Modes, 31. cahier, 20.9.1788, planche II et III, p. 246: Robe à l'angloise and „Negligé du serrail"* (Courtesy Staatliche Museen zu Berlin, Kunstbibliothek, Sammlung Modebild – Lipperheidesche Kostümbibliothek)

# The Motahajiba in Cairo, Inter-Arab Islamic Chic, Adaptations, Hybridity and Globalization

Mona Abaza[1]

The Problem

The post-orientalism debate has obviously influenced feminist discourses on the "orient" in both the metropolises and the global South.[2] The post-9/11 events triggered a wave of Islamophobia clearly latent in the Western world, whereby the veil and Islamic attire turned into a hotbed, or rather the marker deepening the West/East divide. This divide has been articulated by the ideological discourse of the "clash of civilizations." This conflict included heated disputes, drastic policies and decisions which have led to wide-ranging repercussions for the sixteensome million Muslims living in Europe today. The Islamophobic attitude triggered a counter reaction among several scholars who aimed at deconstructing monolithic, essentialist and simplistic clichés of the "repressed,veiled Muslim woman" versus the "emancipated, liberated, secular western feminist."

I agree with Fadwa El-Guindi´s reading[3] of the emergence of the veil in 1970s Egypt as a modern phenomenon, rather as an invention of tradition with no precedent in 1950s and 60s Egypt. I equally agree with her argument that Islamic attire started as an urban phenomenon, to be read as a new form of identity construction and as a movement that advocated a distance from the previous secular, "Westernized" feminists. My disagreement with El-Guindi is in regards to her statement that the movement started as a grassroots phenomenon without really explaining its intricate connection to the regime of Anwar al-Sadat. El-Guindi's statement that the government felt threatened after that the Islamic movement went out of control did, as she has stated, only occur during the end of President Anwar Al-Sadat´s rule. However, what El-Guindi has dismissed in her article is the fact that the Islamic attire was first distributed on Egyptian campuses by the Sadat government to counteract the secularists and

---

1 I would like to thank Lisa Anderson, Provost of The American University in Cairo, for granting me a period of two years' leave that allowed me to finish this work. Special thanks to Leif Stenberg and the Centre for Middle Eastern Studies at Lund University, Sweden, for having included me in their project "The Middle East in the Contemporary World." The Centre for Middle Eastern Studies and the Department of Theology at Lund University were extremely generous in letting me devote all my time to writing.
2 See Entry "Orientalism", Sources and Methods for the Study of Gender in the light of the Post-Orientalism Mona Abaza, Encyclopaedia Women in Islamic Cultures, Edited by Suad Joseph, Brill, 2003.
3 Fadwa El Guindi, Fadwa,"Veiling Resistance" Fashion Theory,The Journal of Dress, Body and Culture. 1999, Volume 3, issue 1, pp. 51-80.

leftists, the two major movements he most dreaded. Sadat felt that he had to counteract, if not suppress them by reviving Islamic sentiments. The record of clashes and deep-seated hatred between the early Muslim Brothers movement and the camp of the secularists/communists dates back to the thirties and forties. We need to be reminded here of Nasser's policies, which violently suppressed the opposition movement of the Muslim Brothers by hanging its spiritual leader Sayyed Qutb and by equally jailing the communists en masse. However, many left wing and secular scholars agree that it was Sadat who revived the Islamic movement when he came to power after Nasser by increasing all forms of religiosity on television and in the press. It was also Sadat who encouraged the banned Muslim Brothers to return to Egypt from exile. He also supported the creation of Islamic magazines like al-Da'wa and al-'Itissam and gave greater power to the religious institution of al-Azhar by granting it the authority to censor books, films and artistic expression. In addition, Sadat declared himself the "president believer" and introduced Islamic Sharia into the constitution, an unprecedented event in Egyptian history. Thus, the whole Islamization of the public sphere did start from the top as a state initiative to fight the then powerful secularists and the leftists on university campuses and in cultural life, leading to the unintended consequence of Sadat becoming a victim of his deeds.

In support of a counter-argument against essentialist visions of the Muslim "un-liberated" woman, it is important to mention the work of Emma Tarlo. Tarlo interviewed three second generation Muslim women living in England, (and in her article "Jenny White"), revealed how nuanced and cosmopolitan these women can be. Tarlo's aim was to challenge the naive association between those donning the Islamic attire with "narrow conservatism". She convincingly revealed that these women are active and creative agents in inventing "stylistic innovations" and demonstrated how their biographies could be read as products of "transcultural interaction".[4] Annelies Moors argued along similar lines but for the specific case of Yemen, whereby she demonstrated how Yemeni attire has undergone global influences, even among the Islamists who abhor fashion.[5] In the case of Turkish styles of dress, it was possible to observe an emerging new Islamic consumerist class expressed in the tesettürlü fashion and lifestyle. Sandikci and Ger demonstrate how, time and again, an interactive process between the local and global is taking place.[6] Jenny White uses the term "Islamic chic" to describe the rising consumerist life styles of the new middle

---

4 Emma Tarlo "Islamic Cosmopolitanism: The Sartorial Biographies of Three Muslim Women in London", Fashion Theory, Volume. 11, issue 2/3 Double Issue June September 2007, pp. 143-172.

5 Annelies Moors "Fashionable Muslims: Notions of Self, Religion, and Society in Sana'a", Fashion Theory, Volume 11, issue 2/3 Double Issue June September 2007. Pp. 319-347.

6 Özlem Sandicki and Güliz Ger "Constructing and Representing the Islamic Consumer in Turkey" Fashion Theory , Volume 11, Issue, 2/3pp. 189-210.

classes.⁷ In summary, it is possible to see a common denominator among Tarlo, Moors, Sandikci and Ger, namely, they all interpret the social actors in these different local contexts as consciously active, modern and positively interacting with the contemporary global markets of consumption.

When speaking of Islamic fashion and Islamic attire, a note should be made regarding the recent debates pertaining to veiling in the European context. Pnina Webner's observation about the paradoxical and often opposing messages and symbols, which have been carried out through the debate as well as the practices, is crucial and timely.⁸ Webner furthermore, points to the phenomenon of the "deterritorialization" of symbols, of religious advices. (the example fatwas issued in Cairo for French consumption. i.e. the issue of the headscarf and Sarkozy), of discourses, of codes of honor leading frequently to a blur, if not a confusion of meanings. The unintended consequences of these actions lead to a loss of sense regarding what it was originally intended to be.⁹ Therefore, interpreting the meaning of the hijab for the second generation post-colonial immigrants, whereby the questions of identity, assimilation, or integration are paramount, is a different story from the emerging new Islamic bourgeoisie and middle classes of the South, which as Webner argued have dissimilar strategies of class struggles that might coincide with a wish to distance one's self from the secular post-colonial past. I quote Webner here: "This echoes Ernest Gellner, who famously argued that: 'Contrary to what outsiders generally suppose, the typical Muslim woman in a Muslim city doesn't wear the veil because her grandmother did so, but because her grandmother did not'".¹⁰

Europeanization

"(Khedive) Ismail was soon to be compared with Louis XIV, but as the Egyptian historian Mohammed Sabry noted "in this court –life after the manner of Versailles, the nobles were notorious foreign adventurers". According to Nubar "France, the Emperor, the empress, haunted the imagination of Ismail as they have haunted that of Said". It was this fatal attraction that was to be Ismail's undoing. He was obsessed with European manners- not so to speak of European women – as he was with European money and European imperial adventurers." (Trevor Mostyn¹¹).

---

7 Jenny B. White "Islamic Chic", in Caglar Keyder (ed.), Istanbul between the Global and the Local. Lonham: Rowman and Littlefield Publishers, 1999.
8 Webner, Pnina (2007) "Veiled Interventions in Pure Space: Honour and Shame and Embodied Struggles Among Muslims in Britain and France", Theory, Culture and Society, 2007, 24: 161-186. Pp. 162.
9 Ibid. p. 162.
10 Webner, p. 173
11 Trevor Mostyn, Egypt's Belle Epoque, Cairo and the Age of the Hedonists, Tauris Parke Paperbacks, 2006, reprinted 2007. p. 42.

Sociological works analyzing the effects of globalisation tend to assess recent transformations in developing societies in the cultural sphere and in lifestyles as newly emerging phenomena, quite often disregarding certain continuities in colonial and post-colonial traditions. If we look at the history of the fashion industry in Egypt, social historians like Mona Russell tell a different story. Namely, that by the late nineteenth century Egypt was a cosmopolitan country. For example, it had a reputation for its cutting edge fashion industry. During that time, Egypt was an active partner in shaping the fashion industry in the metropolises, argues Russell[12]. This role in fashion dates back to the beginning of the twentieth century, owing to the large number of foreign women who "played a key role in fashion transmission providing journals, patterns and stores".[13]

One should perhaps be reminded that the founder of the modern belle époque European Downtown Cairo and paradoxically the modernizer of Egypt, Khedive Ismail (1830-1895) was famous for being a lavish, conspicuous consumer. Khedive Ismail was time and again described as "obsessed" with French culture, its arts, lifestyles and most of all its garments. Mostyn portrays him as a "schizophrenic" ruler combining both an extreme cruelty towards his subordinates, yet possessing a strong wish to reform and modernize the country with the idea of replicating France in Egypt. Khedive Ismail set the example for the ruling Turkish-Circassian classes, which were often depicted as disdainful towards peasants and indigenous cultures. French, English, Italian, or German, became the preferred languages of the elite leaving Arabic as the language of the maids and subordinates. Khedive Ismail´s modernization produced colossal debt, which is often explained by social historians as the major reason that led to Egypt´s colonization by the British.

The adoption of European life styles, the introduction of European furniture, the emergence of salons, the spread of European apparel and fashion, and the preference for speaking European languages, (French, English, Italian, German and Greek) became one of the major shifts of the Egyptian haute bourgeoisie, which shared quite a few characteristics with the foreign communities (of Greeks, Italians, Jews, Belgians, British and French) who lived in Egypt. It seems however, that acceptance into the upper class in colonial times was determined by adherence to particular mannerisms, consumer behaviors, concepts of leisure, and most of all by emulating or simulating closely the mannerisms and hobbies pertaining to European aristocracy.[14]

Egyptian upper classes were for years -and are still- obsessed by branded items. One main aspect of conspicuous consumption was the expectation that

---

12 Mona L. Russell, Creating The New Egyptian Woman. Consumerism, Education, and National Identity 1863-1922. Palgrave Macmillan, 2004, p 30

13 Nancy Mickelwright, cited from Mona L. Russell. Creating The New Womam.p. 30.

14 This point is brilliantly elaborated in Magda Baraka´s pioneering study on the culture and practices of the Egyptian upper classes before the 1952 revolution. Magda Baraka, The Egyptian Upper Class Between Revolutions 1919-1952, Ithaca Press 1998.

upper class members would travel once or twice per year to Paris, Milan or Rome specifically to purchase the last fashions. Meanwhile, classes changed with post colonialism and recently the neo-liberal government agendas, which go hand in hand with a growing Islamization of the society. Along with that fashion also underwent evolutions and mutations. It is possible to speak today of the flowering of a range of fashion(s) in the plural, an observation which I have borrowed from Mike Featherstone when he speaks of the post modern consumer culture that is "based upon a profusion of information and proliferation of images which cannot be ultimately stabilized, or hierarchized into a system which correlates to fixed social divisions..."[15] The implication is the growing blur in correlations made between class and lifestyle. The department store stood as the symbol of urbanity and modernity.[16] If the department store owes its existence to the changes in the production system whereby the factory produced more goods more efficiently, as argued by Richard Sennett,[17] the birth of Egyptian department stores is closely linked with the flowering of Egyptian Jewish capitalism as both Samir Raafat and Joel Beinin argued along similar lines.[18] Jewish capitalism became powerful in Egypt by the end of the nineteenth century. Evidently, Jewish capitalists were the main contributors to the birth of the numerous department stores in Egypt. Les grands magasins carried names such as Ades, Chalons, Chemla, Hannaux, Levi-Benzion, Cicurel (Italian), Orosdi-Back, Simon-Artz, Chalons, Cohenca, Morums, Oreco, Pontremoli, (Salon Vert), Simon–Arzt, and Rivoli.[19]

This list demonstrates that for the pre-1952 Egyptian elite fashion, fashion magazines, the grand couturiers, défilés, and shopping in a francophone grand magasin catered by Jewish origin saleswomen, was typical of the European colonial culture that dominated the modern part of the city of Cairo. As early as the 1930s, fashion magazines portrayed the modern Egyptian woman as being identical to any European modern woman.

I have previously argued in my work on Consumer culture that although Egypt had an early cosmopolitan culture, it was, nevertheless, restricted to the colonial elite and the few who belonged to the landed well-to-do feudal upper

---

15 Mike Featherstone " Lifestyle and Consumer Culture".in: The Consumer Society Reader. Ed. By Martyn J. Lee, Blackwell, 2000, Pp. 94-105
16 Nancy Young Reynolds, Commodity Communities: Interweavings of Market Cultures, Consumption Practices, and Social Power in Egypt, 1907-1961, Ph. D. submitted at the Department of History, Stanford University. 2003.
17 Cited in Peter Corrigan, The Sociology of Consumption: An Introduction, London: Sage Publications, 1997, p. 50.
18 Joel Beinin. The Dispersion of Egyptian Jewry: Culture, Politics and the Formation of a Modern Diaspora. Berkeley: University of California Press, 1998. And Samir Ra'afat, "Sednaoui", Cairo Times, 29 May, 1997.
19 See Historical Society of Jews From Egypt. Department Stores Founded and owned by Jews in Cairo, Egypt: http://www.hsje.org/depstores.htm

class.[20] Globalisation, eventually starting in the early seventies, led to consumerist culture for the masses and consumerism trickled down for the first time in Egypt's history to destitute classes who migrated massively to the oil producing countries and to the poor in slums. Globalisation, eventually starting in the early seventies, led to consumerist culture for the masses and consumerism trickled down for the first time in Egypt's history to destitute classes who migrated massively to the oil producing countries and to the poor in slums.

This was just a prelude to say that what follows regarding "embourgeoisé Islamic chic" ought to be understood as a re-imagined tradition that has no precedents in Egyptian culture.

The "open door policy" launched by the late President Anwar Al-Sadat, was directed towards further American intervention. The massive migration of Egyptians to the oil producing countries and later the neo-liberal agenda of appointing a cabinet of a large majority of businessmen carried on by the Mubarak regime, produced a strong influx of hard currency cash, as well as a massive transformation in the habitat,[21] lifestyles, diet, living room displays and consumer habits for millions of Egyptians. It will not be possible here to delve into the causes of such transformations.

Although consumer culture did provide some semblance of democratization, for instance the spread of mobile phones amongst the poor (who never had access to land lines) and the rich alike and the availability of an improved quality of indigenously produced clothing and fashionable cheap imported Chinese garments, gadgets and household items. Nevertheless, the availability of hard currency cash through tourism and migration to the oil producing countries, far from resolved the class problem. Quite to the contrary, it exacerbated the contradictions through feeding inflated desires and dreams without delivering concrete goods, which were once upon a time delivered by the welfare state to the poor. One thing is clear, cash was increasingly filtered through to certain, previously destitute, classes such as peasants. Whereas on the other hand, a growing class polarization was equally witnessed, with the alarming figure that approximately 40 percent of Egyptians are living today below the poverty line. However, cash and travel diffused widely new lifestyles and made available, as never before to lower classes, consumer goods such as TV sets, satellite programs, refrigerators, washing machines, computers and mobile phones, super and hyper markets and shopping malls, without these

---

20 Mona Abaza, Changing Consumer Cultures of Modern Egypt. Cairo's Urban Reshaping, Brill/AUC Press 2006.

21 The obvious transformation in peasant habitat is the change from mud brick to red brick constructions through the massive migration of peasants to oil producing countries, which allowed them to bring in cash. Thus the traditional mud brick village in the countryside disappeared to be replaced by conglomerates of unfinished multiple stories constructions, sticking to each other in extremely narrow streets. Cairo too looks today like a huge unfinished red brick slum, an observation, which could equally apply to the villages of Egypt.

classes being able to afford to leave their dwellings in the expanding slums. With massive peasant migration to the oil producing countries, a noticeable transformation in apparel (by adopting the Khaliji and Saudi style) was observed, which went hand in hand with a massive Islamization of the public sphere through the growing influence of the Islamic opposition and at a later phase the spread of a conservative middle class consumerist "petro-Islam" brand[22] for the richer middle classes.

This prelude was a reminder that the fashion industry should not be seen as merely an emerging phenomenon of today's globalisation. It should be understood as reactive to the transformations of cosmopolitan colonial culture. As said earlier, if fashion in Egypt has a long history,[23] fashion trends and industries did undergo transmutations.

It is equally possible to argue that during the past decade Egypt witnessed a rebirth in the local fashion industry which managed to conquer European markets and pride for being "glocal". To name a few successful Egyptian brands one can mention Safari, which was became famous for its casual tee shirts stamped with classical comics like Tintin and Mortimer's Secret of the Grand pyramids. Concrete and Mix and Match are two other Egyptian clothing brands that are quite successful amongst the local well-to-do and the expatriate community in Egypt. They manufacture western fashion with interesting adaptations to accomodate local taste and size, (clothes are manufactured larger to fit Egyptians). Marie Louis is yet another success story created by Marie Bishara, a daughter of a textile tycoon. Bishara managed to conquer the Parisian scene in a fashion show in 2008 that was inspired by Pharaonic motives. Here again Egyptomania, and exoticism are certainly a winning card to conquer the French market. Bishara's Fashion show took place at l'Ecole du Louvre to compete with Christian Dior and Balenciaga. Bishara conquered Parisian fashion by re-imagining a so-called Cleopatra dress. Symbols like the key of life and deity Horus were stamped on mini skirts and short dresses, as a marker of difference.[24]

Mobaco is another success story. Created some 30 years ago, Mobaco[25] has gained the reputation of producing high quality cotton shirts made from extra long staple cotton fibres. The factory has meanwhile expanded into producing cashmere, wool and high quality fashionable sport outfits. The owners, a family

---

22 A term that was first used by the Leftist philosopher Fuad Zaquariyya to critique the growing influence of the Pax Saudiana that went hand in hand with the Americanization of Egypt

23 For an overview of the transformation in fashion trends during the Nasser period see my Changing Consumer Culture of Modern Egypt: Cairo's Urban Reshaping. Brill/AUC Press, 2006.

24 Ahram Weekly 23 - 29 October 2008 Issue No. 919, People, Pack of Cards.

25 This information is drawn from the Mobaco Website http://www.mobaco.com/. I have also visited the factory and conducted personal communications with one of the owners of Mobaco in October 2008.

of Armenian origin Egyptian merchants have a long history of trading in textiles in Egypt. The owners of Mobaco are well-travelled francophone businessmen who rarely miss an international fashion show or textile design fair in Europe. The factory is a model in cleanliness with state-of-the-art computerized machinery. The company was created in 1974 as a small factory which has since expanded into roughly 600 employees and 30 retail stores spread all over Egypt. Since 1993, Mobaco has opened three shops in the residential quarters of Paris, (the Seiziemme, Madelaine and St.Germain) The shops are called Mobaco Guichart, Mobaco Tronchet, and Mobaco Cherche-Midi. Mobaco demonstrated that it was possible to conquer European markets through proposing the "uniqueness" of long staple Egyptian cotton and by producing fashionable men's cotton shirts. One can find a Mobaco branch in several international hotels like the Hilton and the Marriott hotel, because it proved to be a success for tourists and expatriates.

The Motahajiba in Cairo

I have previously looked at "ethnic chic"[26] fashion through focusing on NAGADA which successfully started as a revival of an old weaving craft to expand today into an hybrid cosmopolitan mix of tastes that integrated Chinese, Indian, Indonesian, central Asian designs and fabrics to become another international success story. I would like to address yet another style of "Islamic chic", once again, quite internationalized in its production. I will focus on this success story to reveal the variations in the trends of fashion in Egypt. After 9 /11 much attention has been given to political Islam and to contesting Islamic movements. My aim here is to highlight the other facet of the petro-Islam nouveau riche Egyptians. What interests me is the successful marriage between consumer culture and religion via focusing on the increasingly gentrified, middle class life-styles that have borrowed imported apparel and lifestyles from the "khalij"(The Gulf countries).

In the following passage I will narrate the story of the Motahajiba chains in Egypt, as told by a representative in Cairo, Dr. Khaled Ezz Eddin Mahmud. Let us first have a glimpse at how the Motahajiba's main headquarters was opened in Qatar.[27] The Motahajiba is owned by the Al-Siddique International Group, which was created in 1981. The Motahajiba has 23 locations in the GCC (the Gulf countries)[28] and in Egypt. They claim to be the first and only factory in Qatar known to produce the Abaya, the Sheila and the Hijab. They are proud to

---

26 See Emma Tarlo. Clothing Matters, Dress and Identity in India. The University of Chicago Press, 1996.
27 The following information is drawn from al-Motahjiba Website: http://www.almotahajiba.com/other.html
28 The Gulf Cooperation Council (GCC) is an economic block that includes Bahrain, Saudi Arabia, The Sultanate of Oman, Kuwait, Qatar, and the United Arab Emirates.

have more than 100.00 customers and 7500 subscribers. The website states that the Motahajiba caters to the royal family of Qatar, to diplomats and to "the mid high level" customers. Motahajiba has also designed uniforms for large companies and banks. They promote the "height of fashion and class". There is no doubt that the high quality of their products is matched by their high prices.

The initial starting point was the production of the scarf, which was a major success. They then expanded to dresses, Abayas, Cafetans and accessories. The way they advertise themselves on the company website is through their most fashionable dresses. However, these must " conform to the Arab values, customs and traditions, while taking into consideration the Arab Woman's need for practicality in her daily performance at home, at work and at her other activities." The Website also provides detailed manuals and " wearing tips" with drawings explaining how to wear the scarf or the Sheila in a variety of ways. The Motahajiba shops can be found in all GCC countries including the newly opened highly fashionable City Stars mall in Cairo, which is the largest, fanciest and most expensive shopping mall in Cairo.

The Motahajiba in Cairo has gained the reputation for being one of the most expensive and sophisticated shops that sell in vogue Islamic fashion. Most striking is the high quality design of textiles. The highly expensive, handmade, embroidered black scarves could be evaluated as art pieces. They reveal a highly sophisticated craftsmanship. In recent years many former movie stars and belly dancers have re-converted to piety by publicly donning the Islamic attire as a statement. Rumors are that these stars have been paid to do so by the Saudis as part of the pax-Saudiana trend in the Muslim World. Each conversion was mediatised and advertised in the press. Whether these women were funded by Saudis or not, these movie and television stars have succeeded in launching a hip fashion movement, of "Islamic chic" among certain classes. The Mutahajjiba is well-known for catering to those wealthy stars. The shops in Cairo advertise pictures of the converted stars with lavish Islamic attires.[29] I should here make a short note of the fact that Egypt witnessed during the past three or four decades what one can label as the "Saudi Arabization" of garments, daily practices, lifestyles, and the way in which leisure time is spent (e.g. in air conditioned shopping malls). The millions of Egyptians who migrated to the Gulf and oil producing countries have returned with new styles, as well as new imaginations of re-ordering space and sex segregation.

Parallel to this phenomenon, poor Egyptian women were 'sold' as young brides to elderly "Saudi" males often by their own destitute families as a form of disguised prostitution. It became frequent to see Egyptian women wearing the black Saudi Abaya and a face veil as housewives to these Saudi elderly men.

---

29 Television Speaker and retired singer Mona Abdel Ghani appears in the ads of the shop. Actress Hanan Turk who starred in the film of Dunia directed by the Lebanese Jocelyn Sayegh, in the role of a Sufi adept cum belly dancer, adopted shortly after the film the Islamic attire. Both are known clients of the Mutahajiba.

Increasingly, the female "khaliji" outfits were to be noticed in Cairene streets. These were worn by invisible women who spoke Egyptian dialect. Meanwhile, the whole society across classes witnessed an Islamization. A wide range of Islamic attire(s) gained popularity amongst well-to-do classes and in the countryside the face veil, an uncommon phenomenon in the Nile delta, spread rapidly. Segregated gyms and swimming pools and segregated clubs for the rich were created. (remove = reformed their policies). Segregated "Islamic" weddings, time and again another unprecedented phenomenon has been often advertised in websites. Hairdressers and beauty salons specifically for the "muhajjabat" (those wearing the head scarf) multiplied. Islamic department stores like *al-Tawhid wal Nur* chains, in which the staff catering to the public is strictly male , conquered the market to become highly popular for the middle classes. This was just the prelude to explain the reasons why the Motahajiba chain encountered a success in catering to a wider well-off public in Egypt.

A Success Story

"Textiles, on the other hand, are as psychologically basic to human life as food. Biologically, man is a basic creature – 'naked' in the full sense of 'standing unprotected and exposed to the world'. All creatures need a barrier which enables them to resist the changes in the environment to which they cannot adjust. But alone among the animals, the human species has no such adequate natural barrier between itself and the world. Only in the context of this basic situation of humankind can the psychology of textiles be understood.
'Cloth' – a synonym for textile –has the same meaning as ' clothe' –to cover. Naked things, like naked people, demand to be covered. In covering nakedness, whether of people or of things, we accomplish these five basic purposes we protect and insulate; we facilitate contact with the World; we hide defects and weaknesses; we give the appearance we wish to give; and we decorate,..." (Ernest Dichter[30])

I would like here to narrate the story of Motahajiba in Egypt as told by its representative Khaled Ezz Eddin Mahmud. When discussing his family history, Mahmud insisted that he sees two possible narratives to explain his success. (Dr.) Khaled Ezz Eddin Mahmud[31] is a textile designer whose family has a long

---

30 "Textiles, The Fabric of Life, from The Strategy of Desire" (London Board,an 1960, pp104-10. In: The Consumer Society Reader, Edited by Martyn J. Lee Blackwell Publishers; 2000, pp. 229-232. P. 228.

31 The following information was drawn from two interviews with (Dr.) Khaled Ez Eddin Mahmud on the 24 and 27th of June 2008. First in his office in 68 al-Marghani Street, Heliopolis and in al-Motahajiba branch in Kasr al-Nil Street, Downtown Cairo. Khaled Ezz Eddin Mahmud is called Dr by his employees although I am not sure that how he obtained the title. I have also conducted an interview with Mr. Fawzi Rizq Quandil the general inspector of the Motahajiba branches in Cairo on the 24th of June 2008.

tradition in trading with textiles in Egypt. In fact, his forefathers were well-to-do textile merchants in the popular quarter of al-Ghuriyya in the Khan Al-Khalili Bazaar (in the old Islamic city juxtaposing the European Belle Époque downtown). The traditional al-Ghurriyya Bazaar market has been famed for its long history in selling local and imported textiles and fabrics. Khaled Ezz Eddin Mahmud's father and uncles owned the Mahmud Saleh family business. The al-Amir shops owned by the Mahmud Saleh family did very well in the Bazaar before they moved to the modern sector of the city. The family sold their shops in the traditional quarter in the eighties. A shopping mall has been erected on the space of these traditional shops. It is not uncommon to find that many of the wealthy textile merchants of downtown began their businesses in the "traditional" labyrinthine space of the old city of Cairo, to move later to the modern space of downtown, modelled after the Parisian boulevards (called today the Wist al-Balad). Nancy Raynolds' work on the history of first Egyptian department stores at the turn of the century tells a similar story regarding some of the founders of these department stores, such as the Cicurels and the Sednaoui families. Raynolds reconstructs the story of these Jewish and Levantine families to typically reveal a rags to riches epic. She brilliantly traces how the early capitalist accumulation of these businesses started in the Islamic city, then expanded and moved to the European centre.[32] Her main thesis was to challenge the simplistic dichotomy of "traditional" versus "modern" Islamic city versus the modern Haussmannian-Paris-replica, Belle Époque, modern downtown Cairo.

After the 1952 Nasser Revolution and the massive departure of the foreigners (Jews, Italians Greeks and French) from the centre of town, but more precisely after the 1956 tripartite war on Egypt and the nationalization and sequestration of the properties of many capitalists (foreigners and Egyptians), Dr. Khaled Ezz Eddin Mahmud's father and uncles moved to the "modern" Downtown area (Wist al-Balad) and opened two shops, one in the central square of Mustafa Kamel Street in 1957 and another in the again central Kasr al-Nil Street in 1963, just beside the grand magasin "le Salon Vert". Later on, the brothers opened another shop at the then newly opened mall of the Ramses Nile Hilton Hotel. Egypt in the 1950s has been known as the period of Egyptianization (fatrat al-tamsir) according to Mahmud. Egyptianization meant that many foreigners had to leave the country under coercive circumstances, after the 1956 tripartite war and the nationalization policies launched by Gamal Abdel Nasser. The centre of town was mainly occupied by the Egyptian foreign communities.

Urban historians who wrote about colonial Cairo spoke of a split city, of rather, "a tale of two cities". Janet Abu Lughod described Cairo as being a "city and its double". The European, Haussmanian boulevard of modern downtown

---

32 Nancy Young Reynolds, Commodity Communities: Interweavings of Market Cultures, Consumption Practices, and Social Power in Egypt, 1907-1961, Ph. D. submitted at the Department of History Stanford University. 2003. p. 4.

was mainly dominated by foreigners and a few upper middle class Egyptians. The European city was juxtaposed against the traditional bazaar and the Islamic city populated by the poorer locals. Downtown epitomized European culture and modernity, with its department stores, the famed Groppi "chocolatier" and coffee house, its opera house, which was a carbon copy of the Italian La Scala Opera house, French, Italian, Austrian and Belgian architecture, modern cafés, Italian and Greek grocers, and the Azbakiyya Park that was another emulation of the Bois de Boulogne park. This modern world was moving in contradistinction to the traditional Islamic city with its mosques, bazaars, religious schools and historical monuments. One demarcated these two worlds by different smells and apparel- the long male dresses called gallabeyyas/jallabiyyas which were worn by the poor versus the Tarbush and modern outfits and trousers, women in European styles versus the peasants (baladi, local) who were traditionally wrapped in long black sheets.[33] Different languages heard in the streets (pure Arabic in the outskirts of Cairo versus French, Italian, Greek and English in the centre of town) could immediately indicate in which part of the city one was.

The Mahmud Saleh family took over the shops belonging to the foreigners of Egypt in the late 1950s. Thus, Khaled Ezz Eddin Mahmud´s family started to sell textiles in Kasr al Nil Street. He recalls that he started working approximately 30 years ago at a very young age.

After completing a degree in design in 1984 from Helwan University, Ezz Eddin Mahmud started to work regularly at his father´s shop in Mustafa Kamel Street. However, real change occurred in 2000, when, through an introduction by a close friend, he was hired by the Mutahajiba Company in Qatar to become their representative in Egypt. This coincided with the death of his father and uncles. Dr. Khaled Ezz Eddin Mahmud decided then to buy the shares of his cousins and took over the business and the three shops. The Mutahajiba opened its first branch in the residential quarter of Mohandessin in Shehab Street. It was a clever move since downtown had since the late 1980s lost its commercial attraction to quarters like Mohandessin, Heliopolis and the satellite Nasr City. The shop started initially with six workers. Eight years later Dr. Ezz Eddin Mahmud had expanded his operations to ten shops spread all over Egypt, reaching some 300 workers and a creating a factory in Egypt. Today the main office in Heliopolis, designed in the most sophisticated stylish manner, bursting with yuppies and modern-looking employees, can easily compete with any office in New York or Paris. The only difference is that most of the women employed, if not all of them, wear the headscarf. How and why did this success occur in such a short time and without resorting to bank loans?

---

33 Notice that the black long sheet which popular women wrapped themselves with, called in Arabic milayya laff is entirely different from the Gulf Abaya. Egyptian popular women wrapped themselves with it and constantly interplayed in "revealing and concealing" by slipping consciously or unconsciously the sheet down. For this point, see Andrea B. Rugh, Reveal and Conceal; Dress in Contemporary Egypt, Syracuse University Press, 1986.

The answer is simple. When Dr. Ezz Eddin Mahmud opened a branch from the Motahajiba in Egypt, he understood immediately that he had to take the challenge, similar to translating one language to another. It was clear to him that the Motahajiba was selling according to his words a "khaliji/Khaligi sec"[34] taste and Gulf countries designs. This "khaliji sec" needed to be adapted to Egyptian tastes and lifestyles. Fawzi Rizq Quandil, the general inspector of the Motahajiba branch of Egypt, articulates the transformations leading to the success of the Cairo branches differently. He argues that if the Abaya is considered the national dress in the Khalij/Khalij countries, the Egyptians, on the other hand, have no national dress and the peasant "gallabeyya" although fashionable in the eighties among some upper class circles, has not been adopted by female officials in national ceremonies,. The challenge was how to adapt Arab national dress for an Egyptian public. Quandil's answer was two words: "matching" and "adapting" of the Abayas.

Dr. Khaled Ezz Edin Mahmud, on the other hand, states that he quickly understood one main point in fashion: during the past decades women increasingly sought to combine the 'permissible' Islamic attire with their desire to be modern and fashionable.

The challenge was how to propose a modern "chic" dress and yet still be Islamic. It was also clear to him that the Mutahajibba was mainly exporting the black Abaya called in Arabic the Khaliji Abaya.

The Motahajibba was already experiencing a success in the Gulf countries. It was equally clear to him that this is not quite the same taste of the middle and upper class Egyptian women. For example, for Egyptians black is the colour of mourning, which women wear to funerals, and these Abayas were perceived as extremely harsh and austere by Egyptians. "black is not a colour that lends to optimism.. so we had to adapt the Abaya to our culture.. we invented an Egyptian line...we thought of applying international fashion, with the fashionable colour of the year... if mauve or red was in fashion and if fashionable women wore red trousers, then we decided to produce red fashionable Abayas"... Dr. Ezz Eddin Mahmud did include in his team a group of professional fashion designers that brought in the latest ideas and trends. Western fashion was re-adapted to Islamic apparel. They also redesigned the showrooms of the shops. The Motahajiba-Shihab Street shop (in the residential quarter of Mohandessin), is a good case in point for its highly sophisticated interior design.

Therefore, Dr. Ezz Eddin Mahmud decided from the start to revolutionize the designs, the colours and the textiles, in particular the black Khaliji Abayas. He invented new designs, by reworking the fabrics in Bombay to adapt these to the

---

34 The Khalij is the Gulf Zone. All people from the Gulf are defined as khalijis. The French word "sec" has been incorporated in Egyptian slang. Many foreign words have intruded Arabic language .

local Egyptian taste. He stated his doubts that his superiors sitting in the central bureau of Doha would be happy about his alterations, but no one seemed to resist his endeavours. Furthermore, Dr. Ezz Eddin Mahmud borrowed from various styles, such as the Moroccan Cafetan, (which Fawzi Rizq Qunadil differently defines as the closed cut versus the open khaligi Abaya designated in the Gulf as the um-Rashed Abaya, or the croisé Abaya)[35] the Pakistani, and Punjabi designs and perhaps the Malay Baju Kurung (which he himself is no longer sure from where it is borrowed) to come up with an entirely new Egyptian style. In fact, his designs are a patchwork of a refined-reinvented Egyptian-Islamic style. He acknowledges that it is hard for him to give any label to his remake of an "Egyptian Abaya" if he can still name it as such. Embroidery in silver and golden threads (also with beads) were added to the Abaya. Variations in Abayas were produced by adding bright colours. Sleeves were altered in multiple shapes by borrowing from Western fashion. Mahmud states that the Bedouin Abaya has a strong appeal for Egyptians and thus he borrowed a lot from the colours, embroidery and shapes of the Bedouins. Here, the Egyptian peasant large robe called the malass has been also revived and readapted to the Abaya.

Secondly, Mahmud altered the textile production in the Bombay factories that produced for al-Motahajiba. The first thing he did was to use the contacts of al-Mutahajiba to travel to India and get into direct conversation with the factories with whom the company in Doha (Qatar) does business . Mahmud has traveled regularly to India since 2004. He first went to Bombay, then to New Delhi with the assistance of the broker of Doha who took him to the places of production. The Doha Company originally purchased readymade items. Mahmud, by contrast, decided to work with Indian factories on improving and mixing colours that would, according to him, better fit the Egyptian taste. He also noticed that the finish of the clothes was not ideal and he insisted that he did not like the smell of the cloth in India. This led him to take the final process to Cairo and to open another factory. According to him, it was the time when he started collaborating closely with the Indian factories by : "translating our tastes into production" (nutarjim zhawquna ilal muntag). Again according to Mahmud, even if he took Indian designs and the ornaments (zakharafa), he reinvented the combination of colours. Thus a great deal of Indian Organza has been used. Satin was ornamented with embroidery borrowed from the Ottoman tradition using golden thread embroidery (known in Egypt as Turkish Cirma/Sirma work). The Punjabi outfit has been adapted by making the trousers tighter and the dress longer. In fact, he adopted the top of the Punjabi Shalwar kamiz or Salwaar kameez but the trousers were redesigned because they did not match with Egyptian taste. Mahmud says that he has become one of the most famous specialists in this domain with six factories in India (mainly Bombay and New

---

35 However, I checked the Website of the Motahajiba and found that Mahmud's branch is not the only one to adopt the Moroccan Cafetan, but the main company in Doha too.

Delhi) working almost entirely for him. Today, the mixing and customization is done in India and the garments are finished in Cairo.

Third, Mahmud quickly understood that the usage of Indian items, the Abayas and scarves in the Gulf countries takes a different meaning in the way it is worn in Egypt. A Khaliji woman can afford to purchase an Abaya for 2000 to 3000 LE for wearing only in the private sphere of the house, whereas Egyptian women prefer for such a high price to show their Abayas in public. Also, Egyptian women have definitively different definitions of the "public". For example, when an Egyptian woman purchases an expensive outfit, she plans to wear it to parties and on the street. Mahmud was able to grant the franchise of the Motahajiba to found another location in Casablanca. This allowed him to expand his sales and to copy the Moroccan cafetans for the Egyptian production line. In fact, the Motahajiba shops in Cairo have different styles and prices. They also sell entirely locally produced, and evidently cheaper Abayas, besides the Khaliji adaptations, Indian (pseudo-Punjabi) apparel, pseudo-Baju Kurung styles and also pseudo- Moroccan style Cafetans.

Most important is the special crepe and Chiffon scarves (the Tarhas) of the Motahajiba which can be sold for as much as 3000 LE. The Tarha is 28 inches by two meters long. The black chiffon is solely produced in Japan for only Middle Eastern consumption. It is a very special exceedingly dark black colour, which I have only seen in the Gulf countries and in Egypt. The embroidery work called in Arabic shakk (needle work) is mainly undertaken by highly skilled Indian, Bengali and Nepalese workers who stretch the Chiffon on a large piece of wood. Mahmud described to me how he spent hours in Doha watching these Indian subcontinent migrant workers who are displayed to work for the tourist gaze at the show room of the Motahajiba. The refined and sophisticated embroidery is highly celebrated there. These famed Tarhas are to be sold in Casablanca, in Cairo and in the Gulf region for prices which are completely unaffordable to the middle class. Mahmud concluded his talk by priding that his store has won the International ISO (9001) Certificate for high quality environmentally friendly products. He claimed to be the first in Egypt to win such a certificate.

Conclusion

The attempt here was to trace inter-Arab, inter-Islamic adaptations and hybridization in fashion and apparel in contemporary Egypt. The female *Abaya* of al-Motahajiba company in Egypt is an "invention of tradition" which was previously nonexistent. Put in the words of Fawzi Rizq Quandil, its success in Egypt reveals to what extent Egyptians seem to be easily willing to adopt different Arab and Muslim fashions.

This said, these adaptations are not without contradictions and paradoxes. Many Egyptians feel very ambiguous vis-a-vis the Gulf and Saudi "petro-Islam" influence because the millions who worked as migrant labourers have returned with mixed feelings, quite often expressing strong resentments for being badly treated and humiliated as second-class citizens. The 'Saudi Arabization' of the manners of lower classes and of the millions of peasants who have worked for many years there is looked upon with a skeptical eye. On the one hand, the returning peasant migrants have earned money and have improved their standards of living. They have purchased consumer goods and constructed four and five storey red brick houses (often unfinished) for the first time after having lived for centuries in mud-brick dwellings.36 But they also seem to have been exposed to conservative habits that matched with consumerist life styles. They have experienced new forms of gender segregation that were previously nonexistent in Egypt. Here, the Nasserites, the leftists, as well as paradoxically, the ancient regime bourgeoisie, might all be united in expressing similar disapproving comments regarding such an emerging Islamic chic as part and parcel of an overall rising Islamic conservative consumer culture. As stated before, rather than passing moral judgments, it is possible to read the appeal of such apparel as an expression of the desires and wants of the new rising rich and what follows in terms of the changes of lifestyles and tastes. It is therefore possible to see the success of the Motahajiba as catering to emerging classes that wish to differentiate themselves and distance themselves from the former Europeanised and Westernized life styles. The skeptics, on the other hand, see this apparel as yet another form of acculturation no less pervasive than Americanisation of habits and the former Europeanization of the colonial elite.

Bibliography

Websites:
Historical Society of Jews From Egypt. Department Stores Founded and owned by Jews in Cairo,
Egypt: http://www.hsje.org/depstores.htm
al-Motahjiba Website: http://www.almotahajiba.com/other.html
Books and Articles:
Abaza, Mona *"Orientalism", Sources and Methods for the Study of Gender in the light of the Post-Orientalism*, Encyclopaedia Women in Islamic Cultures, Edited by Suad Joseph: Debate, Brill, 2003.
Abaza, Mona *Changing Consumer Cultures of Modern Egypt, Cairo's Urban Reshaping*, Brill/AUC 2006.
Al- Ahram Weekly 23 - 29 October 2008
Issue No. 919, People, Pack of Cards.

---

36 Ecologists would argue that mudbrick dwellings are healthier and ecologically more sustainable. Whereas peasants perceive these as symbolising a pre-modern, retarded state. The wish to live in redbrick dwellings owes a lot to emulating urban 'modern' life, even if these end up looking like slums.

Baraka, Magda *The Egyptian Upper Class Between Revolutions 1919-1952*, Ithaca Press 1998.

Beinin, Joel. *The Dispersion of Egyptian Jewry: Culture, Politics and the Formation of a Modern Diaspora.* Berkeley: University of California Press, 1998.

Corrigan, Peter, *The Sociology of Consumption: An Introduction*, London: Sage Publications, 1997.

Dichter, Ernest "Textiles, The Fabric of Life, from The Strategy of Desire" (London Board,an 1960, pp104-10. In: *The Consumer Society Reader*, Edited by Martyn J. Lee Blackwell Publishers; 2000, pp. 229-232.

El Guindi, Fadwa,"Veiling Resistance" *Fashion Theory*, The Journal of Dress, Body and Culture. 1999, Volume 3, issue 1, pp. 51–80.

Featherstone, Mike "Lifestyle and Consumer Culture".in: *The Consumer Society Reader*. Ed. By Martyn J.Lee, Blackwell, 2000, Pp. 94-105

Moors, Annelies "Fashionable Muslims: Notions of Self, Religion, and Society in Sana'a", *Fashion Theory*, Volume 11, issue 2/3 Double Issue June September 2007. Pp. 319-347.

Mostyn, Trevor *Egypt's Belle Epoque, Cairo and the Age of the Hedonists*, Tauris Parke Paperbacks, 2006, reprinted 2007.

Ra'afat, Samir. "Sednaoui", *Cairo Times*, 29 May, 1997.

Reynolds, Nancy Young, *Commodity Communities: Interweavings of Market Cultures, Consumption Practices, and Social Power in Egypt, 1907-1961*, Ph. D. submitted at the Department of History, Stanford University. 2003.

Russell, Mona L. *Creating The New Egyptian Woman. Consumerism, Education, and National Identity 1863-1922*. Palgrave Macmillan, 2004.

Sandicki, Özlem. Ger, Güliz "Constructing and Representing the Islamic Consumer in Turkey" *Fashion Theory*, Volume 11, Issue, 2/3pp. 189-210.

Tarlo, Emma. *Clothing Matters, Dress and Identity in India.* The University of Chicago Press, 1996.

Tarlo, Emma "Islamic Cosmopolitanism: The Sartorial Biographies of Three Muslim Women in London", *Fashion Theory*, Volume. 11, issue 2/3 Double Issue June September 2007, pp. 143-172

Webner, Pnina (2007) "Veiled Interventions in Pure Space: Honour and Shame and Embodied Struggles Among Muslims in Britain and France", Theory, Culture and Society, 2007, 24: 161–186.

White, Jenny B. "Islamic Chic", in Caglar Keyder (ed.), Istanbul between the Global and the Local. Lonham: Rowman and Littlefield Publishers, 1999.

Fashion in the East: Dress in Modern India

Pravina Shukla

Dress as Material Culture

Material culture, defined by Henry Glassie as "culture made material,"[1] is the study of objects as physical embodiments of culture, recognizing the individual creators and consumers and their interpretations of art and tradition. To understand an object and its makers and users properly, we must take into account several important contexts: the historical time and place of the creation; the biographical context of the artist; and the form, technology, and aesthetics of the object. Proper documentation of these contexts reveals the standards of excellence held by the maker, the consumer, and the society at a particular geographical location and historical time.

My aim over the last decade has been to apply this material culture approach to the study of dress and adornment in contemporary India, an endeavor that has culminated in *The Grace of Four Moons: Dress, Adornment, and the Art of the Body in Modern India*. In studying saris, I utilize the folkloristic model for the study of material culture,[2] with its three key components.[3] First, we must note production: an intervention in nature, the creation of an object that can be alienated from its maker. Second, we look at exchange: a communication between the maker and the buyer, a transfer of the object from one person to another. And finally, we study consumption: when the object once made and sold is now possessed, when this object is not only used, it is employed in a new wave of production, in a second cycle of creation. In consumption, the intervention is not in nature but in culture, when the object is placed within a created assemblage. The art of assemblage, an important creative act in contemporary life, results in arrangements in homes, on altars, and in museum exhibits.

Yet, the most common act of assemblage is that of getting dressed. This takes place daily, perhaps even more than once a day, by most people in the world. By choosing what to wear, and in choosing how to combine dress with ornaments, with shoes, with accessories, with hairstyles, people communicate their cultural

---

1 Glassie, Material Culture, p.41.
2 To read how the folkloristic model for the study of material culture can be applied to dress and adornment, see Shukla, "An Introduction to the Study of Dress and Bodily Adornment."
3 The model, as presented here, has three components – production, exchange, and consumption. It could be reworded to incorporate the three major contexts and categories in which material culture exists: creation, consumption, and communication. To read this argument fully, see Glassie, Material Culture, Chapter 2, pp.41-86.

identity, their historic period, and their personal aesthetics.[4] While no one would question the fact that clothing displays individual and cultural identities, a deeper look at dress reveals the complexities in the production, marketing, and consumption of items of bodily adornment. The study of bodily adornment allows us to further the evaluative model for the study of material culture by adding a final component, that of the interface between the product and the consumer.

Ethnography in the Indian "City of Light"

This essay is based on my fieldwork in the holy Hindu city of Banaras (officially known as Varanasi) in northeastern India, from 1996 to 2003. Banaras is the main pilgrimage site for Hindus because Lord Shiva, locally known as Vishvanath – The Lord of the Universe – rules the world from Banaras. Pilgrims add to the city's population of one million as many as two hundred thousand people a day.[5] The ancient city is a microcosm of Hinduism, and the contemporary city is a microcosm of modern India.[6] Hindu pilgrims visit from all the states of India, and the city contains settled communities of people from many parts of the country. Some pilgrims remain in the city of Shiva, making it their home. Many of those who came from elsewhere continue to practice the styles of their home state and region, making it possible to see many varieties of clothes and jewelry in Banaras that represent the aesthetic and regional choices of wider India. A version of India in miniature, Banaras is a good place to study the interaction between maker and consumer.

Traditional and Modern Dress in India: The Sari

Banaras has long been a center for the production of saris, the unstitched women's garment, consisting of six meters of cloth that is draped, folded, and

---

4 While there are wonderful books on the history and theory of dress, most studies don't analyze how particular choices are made by individuals creating an ensemble. There are a few exceptions. Woodward, in her article "Looking Good, Feeling Right – Aesthetics of the Self" and her book Why Women Wear What They Wear, and also Tarlo in her excellent new book Visibly Muslim all show how a few women make specific choices concerning their dress. Believing self-evaluative comments to be essential to understand the total communication of dress, I devote much time to documenting these kinds of decisions in my book, The Grace of Four Moons.

5 The 2001 India Census lists the population of the city at 1,100,748, just above one million. In the 2002 Road Guide to Varanasi, p.4, the permanent population is listed at 925,962 and the number of daily pilgrims estimated to be from 125,000 to 250,000.

6 Eck, in Banaras: City of Light, expands on the notion of Kashi as the center of the cosmic world in chapter 7, pp.283-303. Cultural geographer Singh, in his book Banaras Region, devotes a section to Varanasi as "the mini India;" pp.66-68.

tucked, in dozens of regional styles. Indians associate Banaras with the exquisite gold-brocaded saris known as Banarasi saris (Figure 1).

Most brides in the country, and in the diaspora, wish to wear and receive for their dowries these lustrous, luxurious lengths of shimmering silk. Banaras's population of Muslim weavers—numbering two hundred thousand according to an estimate by the weaver Shameen Ansari – create the saris in one of the city's weaving neighborhoods: Madanpura, Sonarpura, or Alaipura. Cultural friction between Hindus and Muslims registers tensely in Banaras.

The city is, according to many accounts, about forty per cent Muslim and sixty per cent Hindu. Most of those involved in the sari trade are Muslims, and they have the last name Ansari. My main informants were the brothers Shameem and Hashim Ansari (figure 2), whose workshop, containing sixteen looms, I studied.

Because of the high number of annual visitors, and the local production of saris and jewelry, Banaras has a thriving commercial culture, both wholesale and retail, serving the people of the city, the pilgrims from afar, and the thousands of nearby villagers who come to the big city to shop.

The steady flow of outsiders brings new ideas to the ancient city, ideas that are evaluated, rejected perhaps, or speedily incorporated, maybe by the local women who are visually inspired by an example on the streets, or maybe by the merchants who wish to appeal to the endlessly fluctuating aesthetic demands of their customers. Conservative Banaras makes an ideal place to study tradition in exchange with fashion trends and stylistic diversity.

Weaving Saris

The loom that is used to make Banarasi brocaded saris is a complicated apparatus, joining an old Indian pit loom with the intricate Jacquard loom system of perforated cards that control the design of the woven textile. A French invention of the early nineteenth century, once used extensively in North America to weave coverlets, the Jacquard mechanism is now ubiquitous in Banaras.[7] The weaver sits at the loom, his legs hanging into a pit that is dug two feet deep. Three pedals control the loom.

When a pedal is depressed, it lifts certain warp threads, allowing the supplementary gold-wrapped weft to pass through the silk to create the design on the surface of the sari. When the weaver depresses a pedal, a new card is brought into position above him. Metal fingers poke through the holes in the card, causing some warp threads to lift. The weaver inserts the extra weft by

---

[7] A system that uses punch cards to select a pattern, the loom takes its name from J.M. Jacquard, who patented the device in 1804; Lynton, The Sari, p.197.

hand through this pattern, using separate spindles containing threads in different colors. He follows this with two quick shots of the shuttle, through opposed sheds, binding the fabric together.[8] It takes ten days to two weeks for a weaver to complete a sari.

Although the Jacquard loom seems mechanized, it requires much concentration and skill on the part of the weaver. The master, who sits on the left, controls the pedals, adds the brocade weft to the left border and to the main field of the sari, and passes the shuttle through. He is accompanied by an apprentice, often a younger brother or cousin. The kid imitates the master while working the right border of the sari. The left border, the one created by the master, is continuous, running the length of the sari; it will become the border on the bottom when the sari is worn. The right border does not need to be as long, since most of the right edge of the sari will be pleated and tucked in when the sari is wrapped for wearing.

A sari's excellence depends on its weaver's dexterity, but it is also tremendously affected by the cards that feed through the Jacquard apparatus to lift the warp in patterned combinations. A weaver has to trust that the cards will lift up the correct warp threads to form intricate, beautiful designs. The cards are punched by hand by *cardwallahs*, a set of independent contractors who work for different weaving workshops (like many itinerant weavers, who come and go). Designs, first drawn on paper, and then transferred onto graph paper, are taken to a *cardwallah* who, with astonishing hand-eye coordination, interprets whether a piece of the design needs to be punched in or not, and completes all the cards required to weave a sari in an impressive five to six days.

The most important aspect of the production of saris, Hashim Ansari told me, was the initial conception of the design. Hashim's father, Mr. Abdul Qayoom owns what Hashim calls a "design map," a file containing hundreds of designs. His father consults this "map," lifting designs and mixing the motifs in different combinations to create new saris. Hashim's father invents new design permutations after listening carefully to his son's judgments about the success of saris on the market. Once a new design has been conceived, Hashim's family will hire a designer to render it onto the graph paper for use by the *cardwallah*. There are about one hundred designers available in Banaras—yet another group of independent contractors.

One advantage of a family-run workshop appears in the deliberate division and distribution of skills and labor among the brothers, ensuring an efficiently run business. While Hashim's workshop, like many others, relies on the weavers and *cardwallahs* who work for them, family members accomplish the other important tasks. Assigning titles in English to himself and his brothers, Hashim explained how expertise is divided in the workshop: one brother, Shameem, is the "King of Machines," in charge of fixing the finicky looms; another brother,

---

8 See Barnard, Arts and Crafts of India, for a description and good photographs of Banarasi weavers; pp.136-139.

Hashim, is the "King of Market," buying supplies and selling the saris to shops; the youngest brother, Moshin, is the "King of Dyes," an expert of color combinations and the dyeing of the threads and of finished saris; yet another brother is in charge of the money, paying the workers; and the last, and most important is the "King of Design," their old father, Abdul Qayoom, who invents the designs, and establishes which designs will be woven on which looms in which seasons. When they weave, the masters must keep the female customers in mind, for the season affects both the color of the sari, and its fabric. In the summer months, women prefer the cool of cotton saris in light and pastel colors. In the winter, Hashim weaves darker tones, in what he calls "silk by silk" saris that are silk in both warp and weft. Finally in the transitional seasons of autumn and spring, his workshop weaves light and gauzy silk with georgette, or "china" blends, which combine silk and polyester.

Using the example of the Banarasi sari, we can refine our understanding of the pattern of creation of saris. We see that it is based on an old tradition, and that the tradition is Muslim. The technology is extraordinarily complex, requiring a division of labor. This in turn requires a team of craftsmen, and it requires cooperation among them. There is a hierarchy in production and negotiations must occur on a regular basis.

Buying and Selling the Garments

The first phase of exchange takes place between the maker and the retailer, the middleman who acts as intermediary between the producer and the consumer. In Banaras, shop owners deal with the weavers directly, buying from them at the weekly market at Golghar, or buying from the stock of saris that is walked into their shops on an almost daily basis. Shop owners often haggle to lower the price of a sari by focusing on minor imperfections, acquiring the sari for a cheap price, while degrading its craftsmanship, and insulting the weaver and the workshop.

Sari shop owners, such as Nasir Bhai of Farhan Sarees, often make an initial selection on the basis of taste, and a special collection of these newly acquired saris is set aside in the backroom for shipment to Bombay[9] or other places. Such judgments take place all over the city, being made in the shops for clothing and jewelry, on the basis of some preconceived understanding of preferences linked to caste and regional identity, to urban or rural residence, to economic class and the inclination to follow fashion. Decisions are made by storeowners and clerks with regard to taste and style, and, as a result, an item that a customer in Banaras might wish to buy is left in the backroom or shipped off to Bombay. Another consequence of this practice is that arguably the best things produced in the city

---

9 While "Bombay" is now officially known as "Mumbai," the people I interviewed between 1996-2003 called the city Bombay, still using the old name, which I retain in this paper.

of Banaras are automatically taken out of the city, sent away, destined for acquisition elsewhere.

Nasir Bhai's customers are women, but, Hashim Ansari's—the sari weaver's – customers are men who own and manage sari shops. The weavers must please the men who mediate between them and the women who will wear their creations. Owners of weaving workshops must have an idea of what the sellers want in order to shape their products to please them.

The second phase of exchange takes place between the retailer and the customer, the woman who will wear the sari, incorporating it into her artistic creation of bodily art. By the time a female customer enters a sari shop, a series of decisions have already been made, primarily by the men who have selected the particular pieces available for sale (figure 3).

In the fine stores of Bombay and New Delhi, women shop for clothes much as they do in Los Angeles or Chicago.

They go into a clean, air-conditioned store, and look at the mannequins and through the racks for what they want. In Banaras, as in most parts of India, including the working class sections of Bombay and New Delhi, the style of shopping involves much interaction with the shop owner and workers, who control what the customers see, literally showing each piece of merchandise to every customer, while commenting extravagantly on each and every one.

Most Indians do not view this common shopping style – in which one sits, to be shown the merchandise, bit by bit—negatively. Indians generally want to be shown the clothes and jewelry, while coming into contact with other human beings. There is an unspoken attitude among the customers that the merchant should earn his sale by working at showing—without hurry, and with cups of tea—a representative selection of his stock. Entering a store, women will take off their shoes and sit on the covered mattresses that cover the entire floor of the shop. A salesman approaches immediately, sits across from them, and asks what they want. The clerk tries to get a general idea of what the customer is looking for – price range, fabric preference, color preference, and the occasion for which the saris are needed. After these factors have been determined, the salesman might bring a stack of saris himself, but more likely, he will order a lower-ranked employee to fetch the saris. The sari stock is often limited, based on the current fashion or the season. All colors and fabrics are not necessarily available year-round.

By looking at how the saris are bought and resold, we can generalize about the patterns of exchange in India, a pattern that applies not only to saris but also to other items of clothing and to jewelry as well. We see that the entire process is mediated: the merchant chooses from the stock provided to him by the weaver; the salesman shows the woman the stock designated by the storeowner (for many saris have been pre-selected for Bombay), and then the woman must buy from the selection shown to her by the salesman since she is not allowed to look through the store's inventory on her own, but must sit patiently as the saris are shown to her. There is an initial exchange between the maker and the merchant, and a second act of exchange between the merchant and the customer. This process involves a complicated cycle of choices made by members of different genders, and of various religious and ethnic backgrounds.

Women usually shop in small groups, engaging in what is called "pre-shopping," a previewing of goods with no immediate intention of purchase.[10] While one active buyer shops, her companions engage in a passive act of shopping, taking visual inventory of what is available, storing it for later retrieval. Women choose their saris from within the confines shaped by male taste: first by the weavers, then the buyers, and finally the retail merchants. Yet these men must learn to appeal ultimately to the women who are their customers and whose taste must be taken into account. The customer's experience is mediated, yet there is a reversal of the gender dynamics of daily life. When female customers buy, they are served by men, given snacks, drinks, and attention, being catered to by people of a different gender, and of a different class, caste, and religion (for most sari customers are Hindus). This second cycle of exchange makes women feel served and empowered, asserting their strength as customers, as the final recipients in the process of sari weaving and sale.

Shopping for Clothes

The goal of shopping is to acquire materials with which to create an ensemble, an assemblage, something that is always up to date since it is recreated every time one gets dressed. The sari, made and sold, is now in the possession of a female who will combine it with appropriate jewelry, sandals, handbag, hairstyle, and bindi. The sari is chosen for a social occasion, keeping in mind the woman's age, marital status, social status, religion, body type, and personal aesthetic preferences. When getting dressed, men and women operate within culturally specific notions of gaze and communication. A brief look at two women, Nina Khanchandani and Mukta Tripathi, gives us an example of the kinds of variables and options that influence decisions about items of adornment that the consumer makes.

Nina Khanchandani, a Banarasi, married woman in her early forties, cares little about adornment, and chooses to spend minimal time and effort on her clothing and jewelry (figure 4). But she does not like people staring at her, so, when she goes to a party, she dresses up more than she would like to. At the party, she appears in appropriate dress, her goal being *not* to be looked at. By dressing carefully for the occasion, in the general style, she blends in, and in her words, "stays with the crowd," avoiding extended looks of disapproval or surprise.

Mukta Tripathi, also married and in her late forties, wants, on the other hand, to be the visual center of attraction, and she intentionally dresses a bit differently

---

10 Underhill, Why We Buy, pp.152-153.

from everybody else at a party (figure 5). While, like Nina, she will dress appropriately to fit the social context, she will choose a surprising color, a bold pattern, or a flamboyant style of jewelry. She wants to capture people's eyes by standing *apart* from the crowd. In both cases, these women, Nina and Mukta, present themselves in public, knowing that they will be judged for fitness to social context and in comparison with everybody else's clothing and jewelry. A woman needs to be aware of her dress in relation to others, to fashion, and to the social event, in order to decide whether to blend with the crowd or stand apart in splendor. Either choice assumes she will be seen by others. Given that, she may decide to fade from attention or to demand a long gaze, thereby attracting admiration or, maybe, jealousy. The created ensemble also functions to position women in the relevant contexts that they occupy: social, physical, and developmental.[11]

The last stage in this sequence, that of consumption, centers upon the female customer who is not isolated, but rather, who is operating within a system that always includes men and women, rich and poor, Muslims and Hindus.

In the complicated system described simply in this paper, there are three key players: a sari weaver such as Hashim Ansari, the producer; a sari store owner such as Nasir Bhai, the merchant; and a user of saris such as Mukta Tripathi, the customer. I spent much time with these three people, and they each told me that they believe they are in charge of this linked system of production and consumption. Mukta, as the buyer, believes that with her money she is able to indirectly control the weaver through her interactions with the merchant and her acceptance or rejection of the stock, forcing Hashim to make the saris she wants to wear and buy. Nasir Bhai, as the merchant, on the other hand, believes that he orders the weaver to make only what he will buy, and he also forces the customer to buy what he wants her to select. Finally, Hashim, as the weaver, firmly believes that he, with his family's tradition of sari weaving, has a claim on the art and technology of saris that no one else does. His family makes what they want, hiring the weavers, designers, and *cardwallahs* that they choose to work with, weaving the designs that they have created, drawing from family-owned motifs. According to Hashim, the Ansari family is the one controlling both the merchant and the customer.

Aesthetic Evaluation: Fashion and Beauty

In order to understand the sari in India, we must look at the creation, the exchange, and the use of the textile. The creator, the merchant, and the customer are interconnected in a system that takes into account tradition and innovation, custom and fashion, season and geography, materials and technology, and also

---

11 To read an account of how women, in India and the diaspora, position themselves in time and space by specific choice of dress and adornment, see Shukla, "The Study of Dress and Adornment as Social Positioning.

one that accounts for differences in social status, religion, and most importantly, gender. A final component in this analysis of the sari requires consideration of the assessments made by these key players, comparing evaluative standards to understand not only the connections between the maker, buyer, and consumer, but also to comprehend fully the nature of the relationship between each category of people and the object.

All art is subject to evaluation, both personal and social. In assessment, all the variables that were present in the making of the object come together. The successful product, one representing a perfect combination of technology, materials, and skills, inspires praise or envy from its beholders. The failed product, one deemed to be outside the confines of acceptable aesthetics and form, is rejected or ridiculed.

In examining these aesthetic reactions we gain an appreciation of personal norms of form and function, and also of communal, shared standards of what is acceptable and even beautiful. This examination of evaluative standards accords with the paradigm of performance as it has been successfully applied in material culture study for thirty-five years, in line with Richard Bauman's definition of performance as an act of communication that is artistically rendered in order to be evaluated by an audience.[12] I applied this idea to the study of Banarasi saris by asking the weaver, Hashim Ansari, the merchant, Nasir Bhai, and the customer, Mukta Tripathi, what makes a perfect sari.

Hashim told me that there are many factors that contribute to a sari's overall quality. The most important, according to him, is the design. The designer of a sari must make a host of aesthetic decisions about the motifs and their artful combinations, about the distribution of these throughout the sari, and about the pattern and connection among the designs on the border, the field, and the *palloo*, the elaborate end piece. Though he puts design first, Hashim believes that an excellent sari is also judged by the selection of color and fabric, and by the weight of the sari that results from the choice of fabric and the amount of brocading. All of these features lead to immediate sensory reactions. After the overall aesthetic has been taken in viscerally, the eye focuses more closely on the specific details of the weaving quality, and notes flaws in the execution of the motifs and in the web of the fabric. These secondary technical factors, which might never be detected by the ultimate female consumer, are what the storeowners, the male buyers of Hashim's saris, notice immediately.

According to Nasir Bhai, a merchant, the excellence of a sari is judged by the warp count, and as a result, the degree of fine detail in the design that a high warp count allows. He also believes that the materials should be of high quality: pure silk and real gold threads for the brocading. Nasir Bhai, much like other merchants I interviewed, carefully examines the craftsmanship of a sari: there should be no mistakes in the weaving. The textiles should be smooth, the web

---

12 Bauman, Story, Performance, and Event, p.3.

should not have shading or streaks when it is held up to the light; these result from an uneven seating of the weft, implying that the weaver did not beat down with consistent force. Merchants judge a sari by the quality of the materials, and by the effort exerted by the weaver.

Finally, we turn to the female customer who chooses to buy and wear the saris made and sold by these men. Mukta Tripathi answered my question by ranking sari variables in this order of importance: materials, color (not abstract colors, but the particular hues that suit her skin tone), and only then did she consider pattern and design. She said, as some of the men did, that the first thing to consider is the material of the sari. While the merchants and weavers talked about the quality of materials in terms of an objective assessment of raw products and prices, Mukta, the one who will actually wear the sari, had a slightly different reading of the importance of fabrics. She explained that she prefers cotton, since it feels cool in the summer and warm in the winter. Her second choice is silk, but she only likes it in the winter, since it is too warm for the other seasons. Finally, in the rainy season, she prefers chiffon saris, since cotton, if wet, will not dry quickly, while wet chiffon dries easily under a ceiling fan.

Mukta said that chiffon is the best fabric because it looks good on the body, hugging and enhancing one's shape. In a light, gauzy chiffon sari, the woman's body is on display. A bulky six meters of thick fabric, folded and draped over the body, does not flatter a plump figure. Women, the consumers of saris, emphasize the importance of the fabric for its aesthetic qualities while in use – draped on the body – not for its material qualities as a fabric to be woven or sold.

Taken together these views form a complementary distribution across the field of possible responses to a textile. The weavers emphasize the design of the sari, the merchants focus on the technical aspects of the weaving, and the customers appreciate the feel and fit of the garment. They intersect, differing more than they conflict. It is currently fashionable in scholarship to stress the conflicts and tensions between patrons and makers of traditional arts.[13] The tensions in the art of the Banarasi saris are very real; they result from differences in the status, caste, ethnicity, and religion of the individuals interlocked in the cycle of negotiation. Sari sellers try to unload their old stock on their customers, who in turn try to push the merchants to a low price during hard bargaining. The owners of sari shops lord it over their salesmen. The merchants bully the weavers. The masters of the workshop push around the journeyman weavers, the hired *cardwallahs* and dyers. And always beyond the differences of economy and status, there are the deep-seated religious prejudices that divide Muslims and Hindus in Banaras.

Yet, while people hold different standards of excellence, it does not follow that they are locked in conflict. All of them, though different in gender, caste, status, or religion, operate together within a coherent cultural system. A general aesthetic sense is shared among them. Everyone develops a distinct awareness of the limitations and possibilities within the tight frame of what constitutes a sari, and, in particular, a Banarasi sari. Within this frame, there is breadth enough for a diversity of reactions and creative options, which are, at once, enabled and restricted by the particular technological limitations of this tradition. The standard of excellence for any textile, including the Banarasi sari, includes a grand range of choices in design, color, and fabric, set against mastery of the mechanical demands of the weaving process.

In the case of the Banarasi sari, the male weavers and the female customers, both of whom are artists – the one during textile production, the other during the act of self-adornment – are more forgiving of weaving mistakes than the merchants are. Not being makers of things, the merchants lack compassion for the weaver's difficulties and, perhaps, their need for self-expression, but the merchants have their creative moment, in which many of them are virtuosos – the moment when they sell the creations of other people to the customers who will use them in creative acts of their own.

Conclusion: The System of Fashion in the East

The sari, like all of material culture, is exchanged among people who are often mediating social differences. Banarasi saris move through the differing social classes of the weaver, the merchant, and the customer. They are also transferred from Muslim to Hindu, from men to women. Within this system of the sari, each individual actor has a sense of power. The weaver is the owner of his tradition, in control of his art and its execution. The merchant has power within the commercial realm, asserting his control over his suppliers, workers, and customers. The female customer is in control of her own self-presentation, choosing how to craft her look, answering through her careful assemblage of clothes and jewelry the question of who she is in the world and how she represents herself physically.

The inherent differences among the producer, the merchant, and the consumer interlock in terms of specialization to create social order. This process exemplifies a tradition of folklore scholarship, in which culture appears as a system that allows and accommodates both individual will and social order. The individual gains a sense of empowerment while maintaining the pleasures of membership in a larger entity, belonging to a collective order of the atelier, family, or caste, the regional or religious group, the society and nation united by history and geography.

As a folklorist, I study dress in relation to the dynamic notion of tradition, defined eloquently by Henry Glassie as "the creation of the future out of the past."[14] Tradition is a framework within which one operates. It guides but does

---

14 See Glassie, "Tradition."

not constrict; it allows for individual expression and group cohesion. Fashion, like tradition, is always changing, created anew each time it is performed. Like any traditional act, it is being reinvented within a tight framework of possibilities. Like tradition, fashion is a coherent system specific to a place, a time, and most importantly, a population. Both fashion and tradition are systems understood from within. In Banaras, some women embrace fashion, following it with passion. Other women turn away from it, intentionally rejecting clothes that are in style. Both are willfully reacting to what is currently fashionable. Fashion in their context is not what the West exports. Their local version of fashion can only be understood if we take the time to study the internal system, focusing on the key players through long term observation and in-depth interviews. In this paper we saw how dress in Banaras allows for different categories of people to come together – men and women, Hindu and Muslim, rich and poor; artist, merchant, and customer -- to create social order and a sense of community, uniting themselves by their respective relationship to the sari in modern India.

References Cited

Barnard, Nicholas. Arts and Crafts of India. London: Conran Octopus, 1993.

Bauman, Richard. Story, Performance, and Event: Contextual Studies of Oral Narrative. Cambridge: Cambridge University Press, 1986.

Cohn, Bernard S. Colonialism and Its Forms of Knowledge: The British in India. Princeton: Princeton University Press, 1996.

Eck, Diana. Banaras: City of Light. Princeton: Princeton University Press, 1982.

Feintuch, Burt, Ed. Eight Words for the Study of Expressive Culture. Urbana: University of Illinois Press, 2003.

Glassie, Henry. Material Culture. Bloomington: Indiana University Press, 1999.

"Tradition." In Burt Feintuch, Eight Words for the Study of Expressive Culture., Pp. 176-197.

Küchler, Susanne, and Daniel Miller, Eds. Clothing as Material Culture. Oxford: Berg Publishers, 2005.

Lynton, Linda. The Sari: Styles, Patterns, History, Techniques. New York: Thames and Hudon, 1995.

Niessen, Sandra, Ann Marie Leshkowich, and Carla Jones. Re-Orienting Fashion: The Globalization of Asian Dress. Oxford: Berg Publishers, 2003.

Shukla, Pravina. "The Study of Dress and Adornment as Social Positioning." Material History Review, 61: Spring 2005: 4-16.

"An Introduction to the Study of Dress and Bodily Adornment," in Dress, Costume, and Bodily Adornment as Material Culture, ed. Pravina Shukla, special issue, Midwestern Folklore, vol. 32, nos. 1/2, spring/fall 2006, 5-12.

The Grace of Four Moons: Dress, Adornment, and the Art of the Body in Modern India. Bloomington: Indiana University Press, 2008.

Singh, Rana P.B and Pravin S. Rana. Banaras Region: A Spiritual and Cultural Guide. Varanasi: Indica Books, 2002.

Steele, Valerie, and John S. Major. China Chic: East Meets West. New Haven: Yale University Press, 1999.

Tarlo, Emma. Clothing Matters: Dress and Identity in India. London: Hurst & Company, 1996.

Visibly Muslim: Fashion, Politics, Faith. Berg: Oxford, 2010.

Underhill, Paco. Why We Buy: The Science of Shopping. New York: Simon and Schuster, 1999.

Woodward, Sophie. "Looking Good: Feeling Right – Aesthetics of the Self." In Susanne Küchler and Daniel Miller, Clothing as Material Culture, Pp. 21-39.

Why Women Wear What They Wear. Oxford, Berg, 2007.

Figure 1: Extra weft silk Banarasi sari in the jangli mina design. Banaras, Uttar Pradesh, 2001. Photo by Pravina Shukla.

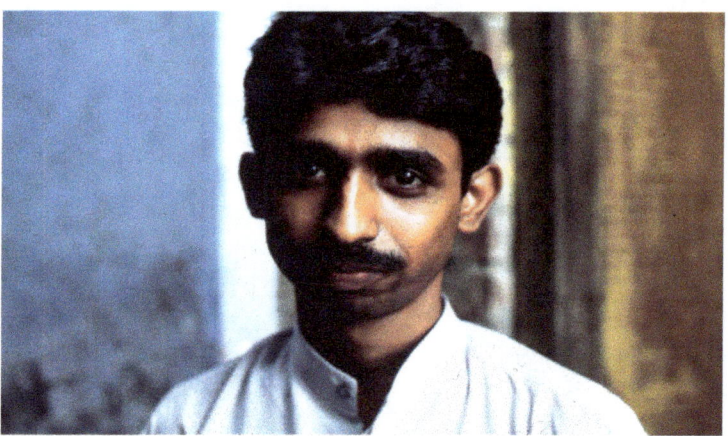

Figure 2: Sari weaver Hashim Ansari at his family atelier, Sonarpura neighborhood, Banaras, Uttar Pradesh, 2003. Photo by Henry Glassie.

Figure 3. Sari shop in Dashaswamedh Road commercial center, Banaras, Uttar Pradesh, 2003. Photo by Pravina Shukla.

Figure 4: Nina Khanchandani outside of her home. Banaras, Uttar Pradesh, 2003. Photo by Henry Glassie.

Figure 5. Mukta Tripathi, outside of her home, Banaras, Uttar Pradesh, 2003. Photo by Henry Glassie.

The Globalization of Japanese Lolita Fashion

Yuniya Kawamura

Introduction

Today's Japanese youth fashion is not dictated by professional Japanese designers who are world famous but is led by middle school and high school girls who have become extremely influential in controlling fashion trends. Since the emergence of the Japanese designers in Paris[1], Japanese fashion has inspired many designers and industry professionals in the West. It is evident on the streets of Tokyo that Japan is becoming the country that can produce unique styles. What is particularly eye-catching is the distinctive appearance of the girls that belong to different subcultural groups that are often female-dominated. A different genre of fashion is being dictated directly and indirectly by these fashion-conscious or fashion-obsessed youths. It is not an exaggeration to say that they are the agents of fashion who take part in the production, reproduction and dissemination of fashion, not only domestically but also internationally. Japanese street fashion emerges out of the social networks among different institutions of fashion as well as various street subcultures, one of which is identified with a creative and original look called Lolita.

A visual investigation of Japanese youth subcultures focusing on their outward appearances is the best way to understand their worldview, values and norms that have changed drastically over the past few decades. The way they dress serves as a marker of social background and subcultural allegiance. Fashion always reflects the prevailing ideology of a society, and today's Japanese youth are the case in point. These teens rely on a distinctive appearance to proclaim their symbolic as well as subcultural identity, which is not consciously political or ideological. The girls claim that it is simply fashion that determines their group affiliation.

I made an attempt to explore Japanese Lolita subculture and its fashion while examining the social and economic factors that may have contributed to the emergence of various subcultures in Japan, including Lolita, and discuss the institutional and individual efforts to spread Lolita fashion globally. This study is based on my ethnographical fieldwork in Tokyo.

Conducting Empirical Research on Subcultures[2]

---

1 For example, Kenzo Takada in 1970, Issey Miyake in 1973, Hanae Mori in 1977, Yohji Yamamoto and Rei Kawakubo of Comme des Garçons in 1981.
2 The study of youth subcultures needs to be conducted not only theoretically but more empirically as well as historically. According to modern theories, subcultures are often determined by class, gender and age and are expressed in the creation of styles in order to construct identities. At the same time, they maintain their autonomy, resist hegemony, exist in opposition to the establishment and construct a cohesive group identity. Furthermore,

I combined direct observation, both participant and non-participant, with structured and semi-structured in-depth interviews to attain unique insight into the world which I examined. I looked at the processes by which individuals define their inner world by their outer attire.

Similarly, I explored the global diffusion mechanism of Lolita fashion from macro-structural and micro-interactionist perspectives. In the 1960s and 1970s, when much of the work on fashion using diffusion models was done, diffusion models were conceptualized as relatively unorganized interpersonal processes, but today, fashion diffusion is highly organized and managed within cultural production systems that are intended to maximize the extent of diffusion (Crane 1999: 15).

Harajuku, one of the fashion districts in Tokyo, is famous for a small bridge near its train station where the Lolita girls congregate. I visited Harajuku every Sunday to become acquainted with the teenage Lolita girls and to interview them. I attended events organized for Lolita such as tea parties and conventions for doll collectors. I also interviewed Lolitas in the US and Italy, both face-to-face and via email, in addition to manufacturers, retailers, designers and salesgirls, who are involved in marketing, commercializing and distributing Lolita fashion.

Structural and Value Changes after Japan's Economic Downturn

After tremendous economic prosperity in the 1980s, Japan's economic bubble burst, and it has been in the worst and the longest economic recession in its history. The situation took a further downturn in 2008 after the Lehman shock. Japanese society was famously cohesive and conformist, but this trend reduced under the strain of economic stagnation. Fathers who thought they had stable and secure jobs were laid off for the first time in their lives, and could no longer be the sole breadwinners of the household. Therefore, the mothers who used to be full-time homemakers had to work part-time to supplement their household income. Japanese companies used to be well-known for their lifetime employment system. That has become a thing of the past.

As a result, the suicide rates among middle aged men soared[3], and male dominance began to collapse. The divorce rate also increased[4]. Companies and families that used to have structured boundaries began to deteriorate. It is not surprising that children found no hope in future Japan. There were widespread feelings of disillusionment, alienation, uncertainty and anger, which spread

---

subcultural theories primarily use case studies in the West, and they are rarely studied transnationally. Cultures and subcultures are globalizing increasingly, and thus the case studies in non-western countries, such as Japan, should not be neglected.

3 In 1998, the suicide rate increased by 34.7% from the previous year, according to the National Police Agency. In 2009, the number suicides increased by 2% from the previous year to 32, 845 exceeding 30,000 for the twelfth straight year. The number among men rose 641 to 23, 471, and those between the ages of 40-69 accounted for 40.8% of the total.

4 In 1993, divorces in Japan reached an all-time high, and the number has almost doubled since 1990. One in every four marriages end up in divorce.

throughout society from adults to children. There was clearly a gradual breakdown of traditional familial, social and economic systems.

The entire society's value system, especially that of the teens, started to change. The previous generation's traditional Japanese beliefs, such as selfless devotion to their employers, perseverance and respect for seniors have disappeared. An intentional shift from old ideology and ways of life are evident. These teens see the assertion of individual identity within their own subcultural community as more important and meaningful than that of a family or school identity which used to be the key concept in Japanese culture. Such attitudes are reflected on their norm-breaking and sometimes even outrageous styles that attract attention both inside and outside of Japan. It may seem ironic, but it is under these social and economic conditions that Japanese subculture fashion became increasingly creative and innovative. The teens wanted to challenge and redefine the existing ideologies, such as the normative standards of beauty and fashion. They are in search of their identity and a community where they feel that they are accepted.

Japanese Lolita Subculture

On the bridge near Harajuku station, for many years, was where many Lolita[5] girls used to hang out. It has been one of the most popular looks since the late 1990s and was also part of the major Harajuku scene. The Lolita style can be seen as a counter-reaction to the Ganguro style and others that evolved out of Shibuya, another fashion district in Tokyo. One of the girls who used to go to Harajuku says: "You would never go to Harajuku dressed in a Shibuya style or vice versa. You would be totally out of place." They know exactly where they belong and how they are supposed to dress. The girls never switch from one subculture to another unless they are cosplayers enjoying their performance.

All Lolita girls told me: "When people see us on the streets or coffee shops, they think we are in a play. They think this is our theatrical costume. That's why a lot of people think this is part of Japanese cosplay, and we are cosplayers. But we are NOT!" I heard this from Japanese Lolitas and American Lolitas over and over again. Cos-play, an abbreviation of Costume Play, is a type of performance in which youngsters dress themselves as their favorite characters in Japanese comics known as manga, or Japanese animated films known as anime. The purpose is merely to have fun and entertain themselves and others, and they often go to various conventions together. Many of them dress as Lolita because these characters appear in manga and anime. However, for the authentic Lolitas, it is highly offensive for them to be called a cosplayer. Lolita plays an important part of their life, or sometimes, it consumes their entire life. One of the Lolita

---

5 The term 'Lolita' reminds Westerners of the novel written by Vladimir Nabokov in 1955, but during my research, I did not come across one single Lolita individual who knew about the book. Japanese Lolita is not the sexually precocious child that appears in the novel.

girls said: "I am constantly thinking about Lolita. It is my whole life and identity."

The population of Lolita on the Harajuku bridge started to decline in the past few years, and some may claim that this is a sign that the subculture is gradually dying out. On the contrary, those who used to hang out there were the fans of the Visual-kei musicians with heavy make-up and flashy outfits, and they are not real Lolita. The real ones are here to stay.

Like many other subcultures in Japan, Lolita is dominated by girls, and it projects the image of a Victorian doll with pale or fair skin, curly blonde or brown hair, knee- or mid-thigh-length dresses with lots of lace, ruffles and frills, pinafores, bloomers, stockings and flat shoes or boots. The followers create and use their own language and abbreviations that outsiders cannot comprehend, such as Loli-bra which means a Lolita brand or a cardi which means a cardigan. They are bound together by their stylistic expressions, and many have created website communities.

Unlike the Gyaru and Gyaru-o subcultures found in the Shibuya district that put an end to their membership after several years when they reach a certain age, Lolita has no graduation age or date. They can go on for life if they wish. According to one of Lolita girls that I interviewed, "You can remain a Lolita as long as you don't have wrinkles around your eyes".

Various Genres of Lolita

Lolita has branched out into different subgroups:

Gosu Loli (Gothic and Lolita): the combination of Gothic and Lolita elements; monochromatic palette, often black and white.

Punk Loli (Punk Lolita): the combination of Lolita and punk elements such as leather, zippers, safety pins and chains (Figure 1).

Ama Loli (Sweet Lolita): the typical Lolita style with lots of lace, ruffles and frills; mostly pastel colors, such as white, blue and pink.

Classic/Elegant Lolita: similar to Ama Loli (Sweet Lolita) but with fewer ruffles and frills (Figure 2).

Hime-Loli (Princess Lolita): similar to Classic Lolita: pastel colors; princess accessories, often with a tiara.

Pinku Loli (Pink Lolita): pink from head to toe.

Kuro-Loli (Black Lolita): black from head to toe.

Wa-Loli (Japanese Lolita): Lolita combined with traditional Japanese elements, such as kimono and obi.

Futago Loli (Twin Lolitas): two girls wearing the exact same style.

Each genre has its own distinctive style and rules that the followers adhere to. Lolita is not simply fashion, but has become a subcultural lifestyle, and this particular subculture has spread worldwide among teens in the U.S., Europe and Asia. While some belong to a specific Lolita category, others enjoy choosing different styles based on the occasion. Some Lolitas impose strict rules on as to what is really considered authentic Lolita, and there are heated discussions on the Internet message boards.

The Global Diffusion of Japanese Lolita

Whether it is authentic Lolita or part of cosplay, Lolita fashion is beginning to take root around the world. Diffusion theories of fashion seek to explain how fashion is spread through interpersonal communication and institutional networks, and they assume that the fashion phenomenon is not ambiguous or unpredictable. Diffusion theories of fashion can focus on individuals, which give a small-scale analysis, and on institutions, which provide a systematic, large-scale approach. Similarly, fashion subcultures can be studied either on an individual basis, as in psychology, or may view the structure and function of society as a whole, as in sociology.

Thus, we can see individuals and institutions involved in the diffusion process of Lolita. The source of fashion diffusion used to be a highly centralized system, initially found in Paris. Innovators belong to a community where a group of individuals and organizations are involved in the production, reproduction, evaluation and dissemination of a specific form of culture as well as subculture. Opinion leaders and gatekeepers included editors of leading fashion magazines and highly visible fashion consumers, such as society women, movie stars, and popular music artists (Crane 1999: 16). Today, however, the centralized fashion system has been replaced by a new system. Trends are no longer set solely by professional designers. Fashion originates in many types of social groups, including adolescent urban subculture, and consequently, fashion emanates from many sources and diffuses to different publics (Crane 1999: 13).

Institutional Efforts
There are several institutional efforts to spread Japanese Lolita worldwide, and it appears to be one of the most well-known Japanese subcultures overseas. The Japanese government, in addition to profit and non-profit organizations, realizes that there are significant commercial potentials to Lolita.

In March 2009, the Ministry of Foreign Affairs appointed three Kawaii (cute) Ambassadors, Shizuka Fujioka, Yu Kimura and Misako Aoki. They went around the world promoting Japanese Kawaii culture worldwide. According to their press release (2009),

The main mission of the three ambassadors is to transmit the new trends of Japanese pop culture in the field of fashion to the rest of the world and to promote understanding of Japan by their attending cultural projects carried out by the Japanese Embassies and the Japan Foundation. Pop culture, including fashion, is an integral part of today's Japanese culture. It enjoys worldwide popularity and we witness that such people are ever-increasing. Pop culture is expected to help the people of the world have more chances to know about contemporary Japan, hand-in-hand with other traditional and contemporary cultures.

Fujioka gave a lecture on Japanese fashion at the Japan Festa in Bangkok in March, 2009. Of the three, Aoki, a Lolita model for the two major magazines, Gothic and Lolita Bible and Kera, went to The Japan Expo in Paris to promote Japan's pop culture diplomacy. Aoki was also sent to Brazil to attend the World Cosplay Summit to introduce Lolita fashion in addition to Italy, Spain, Korea and Russia.

Many European Lolitas visit The Japan Expo in Paris which is one of the world's largest international events celebrating Japanese pop culture, where over 160,000 people interested in Japanese pop cultural trends gather from all over the world (Figure 3). There are trade fairs, fashion shows, games, and various events related to Japanese popular culture, including Lolita. The Ministry of Foreign Affairs (MOFA), the Agency for Cultural Affairs, the Ministry of Economy, Trade and Industry (METI) and the Japan Tourism Agency (JTA) collaborated to participate in the Japan Expo Paris 2010. The number of visitors has been increasing every year since its inception in 2000. The Lolitas travel primarily from European countries, such as Germany, Spain, and Italy, and have meet-ups at the convention.

Furthermore, the Fashion Institute of Technology in New York hosted a Lolita tea party in October, 2010, in conjunction with its exhibition Japan Fashion Now! featuring contemporary Japanese fashion from world famous designers such as Issey Miyake and Yohji Yamamoto, to youth subcultural fashion, including different styles and brands of Lolita fashion. A new store Tokyo Rebel opened in New York in 2009 that exclusively sell imported Japanese Lolita fashion (Figure 4 and 5).

Individual Efforts

Many Lolita followers in Europe and the US have never been to Japan, but they are fascinated by the style. On an individual basis, it is undoubtedly the Internet that has been the key tool that helps them find information about Lolita fashion, events, auctions, and chat rooms. Many are initially influenced by manga and anime, and come to Lolita fashion soon after. Had it not for the invention of the Internet, Lolita would not have spread this quickly and widely.

A twenty-two-year-old Italian Lolita (Figure 6) who has been wearing Lolita since 2006 said: "The first time I found Lolita was on the Internet. I was looking for an image of a manga that I was reading. Then I started to get more information about this subculture, and I found an Italian forum about Lolita (gothiclolita.forumcommunity.net)." An American Lolita also told me: "I went to a Japanese bookstore with my friends and found Gothic & Lolita Bible and fell in love with it. Then I started to google to get more information on the Internet."

They find sufficient information online about Japanese Lolita brands that they want to wear. They are familiar with almost all the well-known Lolita brands, such as Baby Stars Bright Shine, Metamorphose or Angelic Pretty.

The Italian Lolita girl continued: "My favorite brand is Alice and the Pirates, but I love Innocent World and Mary Magdalene, too. Usually I buy them through international online shops, but sometimes I also buy secondhand through European Lolita girls. I can buy them in Italy, too, but there are few shops that carry them, and their prices are really high, usually three or four times the original price in Japan so I prefer to buy them online." The Lolita clothes are rather expensive, and it is probably one of the reasons why many Lolitas sew their own clothes.

It is not only the look that they adopt but also a lifestyle. Lolita girls like to organize tea parties, and often find their friends in Internet chatrooms or social networking sites and meet in person at the parties. There is a large American Lolita community on Live Journal (www.livejournal.com), a popular social networking site, and it is subdivided into smaller communities with specific Lolita interests, such as Lolita Housewife, Princess Lolita, Loli Graphics, Lolita Indies, and Lolita Pattern Swap among many others. There is a Lolita community almost in every state in the U.S. One of the largest Lolita communities on Live Journal writes:

Welcome to The Elegant Gothic Lolita (EGL) Community! Please make sure and understand all the rules before posting! Our mission is help others share, grow, and learn in the Gothic Lolita fashion. The community discussions focus on Japanese Gothic Lolita fashion and its manifestations the world over. We hope you will enjoy browsing our community!

The community has monthly themes. For example, the general theme for October is Lolita & Literature. Participants can share some writings of their own, or they can show a co-ordinate inspired by their favorite novel, they can recommend the literary Lolita. They also have the Aesthetic Theme and for October, it is Sombre: encouraging participants to show the dark and scary side of Lolita, and "If it's gloomy, it's good to go".

From Collective to Individualistic Identification within Lolita Subculture

While conventional youth subcultures such as British punk or American inner city hip hop often convey a strong political or ideological statement, the Japanese teens claim that they have no message and say that their distinctive style is pure entertainment. Looking for fashion which makes them cute is of utmost importance since they want to stand out and be noticed. The teens that belong to the subcultures are always with friends who dress in similar fashion.

Fashion is a representation of one's inner self as well as one's group affiliation. Having no message to convey already conveys a message.

Muggleton (2000), who supports postmodern theory, explains that subcultures today exist in postmodern form. His idea of postmodern subculture involves a combination of hybridity, diversity and fluidity. According to Muggleton (2000: 15), traditional points of collective identification such as class, gender, race and place, are gradually replaced by elective, build-your-own, consumer identities, and the members of subcultures are postmodern in that they demonstrate a fragmented, individualistic and stylistic identification. This is a sensibility that manifests itself as an expression of freedom from structure, control and restraint, ensuring that stasis is rejected in favor of movement and fluidity (Muggleton 2000: 158).

Style differentiation no longer defines different social classes. There is a great deal of interclass and intra-class mobility. Social identity that used to be based on economics and politics is now based on something outside of these spheres. The consumption of cultural goods, such as fashionable clothing, performs an increasingly important role in the construction of personal identity, while the satisfaction of material needs and the emulation of superior classes are secondary (Crane 2000). According to Crane, we see a shift from class fashion to consumer fashion. In postmodern cultures, consumption is conceptualized as a form of role playing, as consumers seek to project conceptions of identity that are continually evolving. Social class is less evident and important in one's self-image and identity in contemporary society than before.

These Lolita girls are playing the role of a princess. The Italian Lolita girls said: "I like the feeling when I look at myself at the mirror with Lolita clothes. I may be naive, but I really feel like a princess. I love it. I like the Lolita culture too, but probably because it suits my usual way of acting and thinking. If I'm dressed like a princess, I act even more properly like a lady."

A Japanese Lolita who wears it on weekends also remarked: "When I dress Lolita, it changes my demeanor. The way I talk. The way I walk. Everything about me changes. I feel like a princess." She goes to Butler Café where waiters are dressed as English butlers and treat their female customers like princesses. She continued: "I love coming to this café, because I am treated like a true lady. This is real me. When I am not dressed Lolita, that's not me. Lolita is real me. When I put on a Lolita dress, I am thinking to myself which look do I want today? After deciding that I want to go Ama-Loli, then I put all the accessories together to make that look. That thinking process itself and turning into a princess are great fun."

In Japan, Europe or the US, the girls are all aware that the Lolita style is often perceived as strange, and people turn their heads when they walk on the streets. The Japanese Lolita said: "If my boyfriend doesn't like me in Lolita, I would rather break up with him than change my style."

Conclusion

Lolita subculture that used to be known only locally is now going global. Subcultures are becoming borderless and are spreading to every corner of the world since the majority of the people have access to them through the Internet. The exclusive Lolita look in any country functions as a visible group identity for the teens, creates the bond and becomes a shared sign of membership affiliation. It is also used to communicate their ideas, intentions, purposes and thoughts. These styles are functional and purposeful only within the specific symbolic territory among particular groups of people. The Lolita girls rely on a distinctive appearance to proclaim their subcultural identity by which they define themselves. It is the ultimate self-expression for those who assert their social selves.

References

Crane, Diane (1999), 'Diffusion Models and Fashion: A Reassessment in the Social Diffusion of Ideas and Things', The Annals of the Academy of Political and Social Science, 566, November: 13-24. (2000), Fashion and Its Social Agendas: Class, Gender, and Identity in Clothing, Chicago, IL: The University of Chicago Press.

Kawamura, Yuniya (2004), Fashion-ology: An Introduction to Fashion Studies, Oxford, UK: Berg.(2006)

'Japanese Teens as Producers of Street Fashion', in Patrik Aspers and Lise Skov, Current Sociology, Volume 54, Number 5, September, pp.784-801, Thousand Oaks, CA: Sage. (2007)

'Japanese Designers in Postmodern Times', in Ian Luna (ed.), Tokyolife, pp.140-43, New York: Rizzoli.

Ministry of Foreign Affairs (2009), Press Release: Commission of Trend Communicator of Japanese Pop Culture in the Field of Fashion, February 25.

Muggleton, David (2000), Inside Subculture: The Postmodern Meaning of Style, Oxford UK: Berg.

Figure 1: Punk Lolita in Tokyo: Model-Sara; Photo-Courtesy of Kera Magazine

Figure 2: Classic Lolita in Tokyo: Model-Manami Abe; Photo by Masato Imai

Figure 3: Sweet Lolitas in Paris; Photo-Courtesy of Tenkai-Japan.

Figure 4: Sweet Lolita in New York; Photo by Yuniya Kawamura

Figure 5: Sweet Lolita in New York. Photo by Yuniya Kawamura

Figure 6: Elegant Gothic Lolita in Treviso, Italy: Model- Silvia Nodari

even
Reviving Kimono. Fahion as Memory at the Turn of the Twenty-First Century

Oly Firsching-Tovar

Introduction

Since the end of the 1980s the *yukata* (informal cotton kimono) gradually regained popularity between the young Japanese generation, first among the girls but soon the boys followed, too. Used as a light cotton kimono for the summer season or as pajamas after taking a bath at Japanese hot springs, the *yukata* has made a comeback, updated as a fashionable, everyday kimono. Influenced by the changing trends in textile design created by different kimono magazines, Japanese and Western fashion designers, the Japanese apparel market and department stores, the *yukata* is worn today for parties, shopping, for dates or for the celebration of various summer festivities, like *hanabi* (fireworks) or traditional festivals as the *Gion Matsuri* in Kyoto.

It is no longer possible to imagine the events of the hot season without wearing a *yukata*, and so the *yukata* can be considered the first step that young Japanese people take in order to learn how to wear the more complex kimono. Although the tradition of wearing kimono in the everyday life has almost died out along with the rapidly advancing economic growth of Japan after World War II, the garment has experienced a comeback in the last ten years[1]. Nowadays there are plenty of opportunities to get dressed up as a *geisha* and to visit special shops in tourist areas of Tokyo or to travel to a traditional city like Kyoto in order to rent a kimono and take pictures in beautiful Japanese scenery during the autumn. On these occasions the contemporary Japanese youth enjoys his country and ethnicity. I had the chance to observe these phenomena while doing fieldwork in Japan.

During the field work as part of the empirical research for my doctoral thesis on kimono revival and recycling in contemporary Japan, I visited bookshops and kimono boutiques in Kyoto and Tokyo. There I found several newly-published books, booklets, *mooks* and magazines on the themes of kimono and of tourism in Kyoto, published in Japanese language and printed in Japan after the year 2000. The "*mook*", a magazine-style book that is popular in Japan, attracts the target audience especially well. The style of the presentation and concept of these publications can be considered lighthearted and is easy to read and understand; they are fully illustrated with pictures, maps, and short texts for the

---

[1] To see more information on the comeback of the kimono culture in contemporary Japan look at Stephanie Assmann essay: Between Tradition and Innovation: The Reinvention of the Kimono in Japanese Consumer Culture.

targeted consumer, primarily young people interested in the field of contemporary kimono culture and in Kyoto.

Considered the heart of Japanese traditions, Kyoto is also a cosmopolitan cultural center where elements of Japanese traditions and Western modernity blend. Is Kyoto then the place to re-discover traces of the époque of creative fusion of Japanese tradition and Western modernity?

This question arises with the founding and analysis of the *mook* "*Kimono at Kyoto*" that I obtained during my fieldwork in Japan in year 2008. In this publication, the nostalgia for better times of Japanese modern society, like the era called *"Taisho Romanticism"*, seems to be romanticized while recalling modern kimono fashions and by touring Kyoto´s juxtaposed environs of traditional Japanese and modern Western style of architecture.

Current scholarship on the history of modern kimono also studies the connection of tourism, Orientalism and marketing strategies for kimono fashions. Orientalism[2] as a science has constructed an image of Asia as an exotic, timeless, passive and feminine part of the world that never changes and which is inferior to the West. Concerning Japanese culture one of the stereotypical images of exoticness is usually the kimono-clad maiden. Sometimes this image is consciously used inside Japan to reinforce its ancient and exotic cultural heritage.

One of such cases has been studied in the introduction of Terry Satsuki Milhaupt essay "Facets of the Kimono: Reflections of Japans Modernity"; published in the Arts of Japan: The John C. Weber Collection, edited in year 2006[3]. Milhaupt analyzed the frontispiece of a book edited in 1936 by the Japanese Government Railways and the board of Tourist Industry.

Milhaupt's thesis is that this book was intended to promote the kimono ideal as a symbol of "traditional" Japan for western travelers4. Her investigation reveals elements of Orientalism - 'the Orient within', reworked by the Japanese Government that tried to accentuate the timeless quality of kimono to attract foreigners to Japan. In this essay I look at Milhaupt's proposal in the review of the history of modern kimono in regards to how the term kimono became synonymous with "Japanese Dress" in order to evaluate the possible and current Orientalist strategies at play in the way kimono have been revived in contemporary Japan.

"Kimono at Kyoto"

The cover picture of the mook named "Kimono at Kyoto" served as the key inspiration for the writing of this paper (figure 1), its eclectic design is a mix of Art Nouveau romantic decoration and bright flat squares of colors in red, purple,

---

2 Said EW, 1979
3 Trede M, 2006.
4 Milhaupt, Terry Satsuki, 2006, p.p.34.

yellow and pink reminiscent of Art Deco. The red square of the cover is the frame of a picture portraying two young Japanese girls dressed in casual kimonos talking in a western building interior. In the yellow and purple squares the title of the publication "Kimono at Kyoto" is written in a combination of katakana alphabet (used to translate foreign languages) and roman letters using the English preposition "at" to give an attractive foreign touch to it. As an incentive to buy the book, the reader receives a short invitation to walk in Kyoto to do some shopping for kimonos while getting to know the artist, designers and kimono coordinators that live and work in the city today. Kyoto as the epicenter of this tourist attraction appears in this publication as well as in Dorinne Kondo's essay "The Orient Within: Kyoto Etrangere"[5] in About Face as "a metonym for authentic tradition and renewal for the postmodern Japanese".

"Kimono de Osampo"

The chapter titled "Kimono de Osampo" which means "to go for a walk or make an excursion while dressed in a kimono" gives advice to Japanese tourists suggesting unusual, impressive visits that one could make around Kyoto city center. The girls in chapter three are in charge of leading the tours. The first walk accompanies two of these girls on their journey through Kyoto which also seems to be a journey in time. The set of kimono and obi one of the girls wears is complemented with a flower motif hanakazari worn to the side in her hair in coordination with a knitted shawl; these accessories recall past kimono fashions, specifically the way some women looked with their kimonos during the Taisho era (1912-1926)[6]. In (figure 2) a poster advertises the autumn and winter collection at a second-hand kimono boutique, featuring the model in a contemporary interpretation of the Taisho kimono look.

The next recommendation is to visit the historical street of Sanjo, one of the main streets of Kyoto's modern architecture with its retro atmosphere and pedestrian walkways; it is also suggested that the spirit of the famous Japanese women of the Taisho era the "Modern Girl" and its energy can be felt while walking the tour through the streets.

This second tour starts with the sight of a temple where a stylishly-clad couple is standing facing one another, flirting, in modernized kimono outfits. The girl has dyed brown hair and the boy also has a contemporary haircut; their chic kimonos are designed in a cool color palette of black, white, purple and mouse grey. Contrasting with their outfits the scenery (the side of the wall of a temple) a historic atmosphere of a temple, the essence of Kyoto condensed in such a historical site; this rather atypical scene accentuating the mix of

---

5 Kondo DK, 1997, p.p. 80.
6 According to Dalby: Knitting enjoyed a tremendous vogue around 1918, soon manifesting itself in the sudden popularity of sweaters and shawls for women. Dalby, Liza 2001.p.p. 140.

traditional and modern elements. The temple and kimonos stand for tradition, the way the models interact in their kimonos and their liberated and rebellious "looks" stand for modernity and emancipation from the conservative kimono rules and etiquette.

According to the guide nightlife and kimono are connected in Kyoto. The guide depicts a single girl appearing at a bar and at other places around Kyoto's city center; restaurants, pool bars and also a club with a DJ and a cafe are advertised. "Taisho Romanticism" as an artistic and literary movement in the Taisho period of Japanese modern history is recalled in this chapter as a "Retro-Modern Style" and the young girls that are used as models and who toured alongside the reader within the pages are associated in the written text of the book and to some extent with the style of their kimonos and accessories with the "Modern Girls", Japanese young women and western style fashion trend setters of the 1920s.

This raises the question: Could a kind of "Memory Culture" in the sense of Jan Assmann7 on "Taisho Romanticism" (1912-1926) and on modern kimonos being consciously revived as a strategy by which Japanese young girls and boys can enjoy contemporary kimonos while making a trip to the past by visiting Kyoto?

Who were the "Modern Girls" of the Taisho period? What were the characteristics of the kimono then? What kind of Orientalist strategies try to make the "Modern Girls" of bygone days, once the pioneers of Western fashion in Japan, an archetype of fashion for kimono today?

Kimono: Japanese Dress

In the world kimonos are known as the National Dress of Japan and the Japanese themselves recognize their kimonos as dress that represents their culture and its uniqueness among nations. Moreover as anthropologist Liza Dalby8 explains:

"The kimono that today claims the title National Dress of Japan is the ensemble of silk robe and brocade obi that a modern Japanese woman thinks of as a ceremonial alternative to a dress on her home turf-or as a way to impress foreigners when abroad. This kimono is the outfit in which a young woman chooses to be photographed for her official marriage dossier portrait. This kimono is preferred dress for entrance ceremonies, graduations, and cultural pursuits where feminine character is on display"

---

7 After Jan Assmann: Memory Culture is the way a society ensures cultural continuity by preserving, with the help of cultural mnemonics, its collective knowledge from one generation to the next, rendering it possible for later generations to construct their cultural identity. Assmann, Jan, 1992, p.p. 30-34.

8 Dalby, Liza, 2011, p.p.127.

As explained in the work of Terry Satsuki Milhaupts in year 2006 the term "kimono" is a modern invention, she agrees with the anthropologist Liza Dalby[9]:

"It was primarily in response to the influx of Western-style clothing in the mid-nineteenth century that the Japanese first recognized the significance of their distinctive mode of dress"

Dalby places the discovery of the term kimono at the end of the nineteenth century[10]:

"It took most of the momentous half century of the Meiji emperors' reign (1868-1912) for Japanese clothing to focus on the kimono and to define itself as such"

Kimono means literally "a thing to wear" and the garment was commonly known as kosode, a garment with small sleeve openings. Milhaupt writes that the stereotypes of static traditionalism attached to the garment have been constructed[11] by the Japanese themselves. Her thesis is that the kimono not only stands for Japanese tradition but also that kimono of the Meiji, Taisho and early Showa periods corresponding with the years between 1868 and 1940s reveals the influence of the capitalistic system of production, design and marketing of kimonos as consumer goods. In this way kimonos as a commodity that "had a useful quality"[12] were important in the process of modernization in which Japan was involved since its opening to the West with the Meiji Restoration (1868-1912).

As an example on how kimono image as "Japanese Dress" had been constructed, Milhaupt cited a book published in 1936 by the Board of Tourist Industry and Japanese Government Railways[13]. The publication that targeted "the foreigners interested in Japan", was named "Kimono: Japanese Dress"[14]. Its author, known as Kawakatsu Ken ichi, was a managing director of the famous Takashimaya department store[15]. The goal of the book as edited in collaboration with the Japanese government was to promote the idea of the kimono as a symbol for Japanese Dress in the West[16].

---

9 Milhaupt, Terry Satsuki, 2006, p.p.34.
10 Dalby, Liza, 2001, p.p.65.
11 Milhaupt, Terry Satsuki, 2006. p.p.34.
12 Oxford English-English E-Dictionary.
13 Milhaupt, Terry Satsuki, 2006. p.p.34.
14 Milhaupt, Terry Satsuki, 2006. p.p.34.
15 Milhaupt, Terry Satsuki, 2006. p.p.34.
16 Milhaupt, Terry Satsuki, 2006. p.p.34.

"A WOMAN WITH stylishly bobbed hair and kimono-clad figure admires her reflection in a full-length mirror. Her photograph serves as the frontispiece to Kimono: Japanese Dress"[17]

This idea of promoting the kimono as "Japanese Dress" in the West to attract foreign travelers may have started with the participation of Japan in the World International Expositions as it was around the end of the 19th century that the term "kimono" became part of the western lexicon. Akiko Fukai states that "according to the Le Grand Robert dictionary, the word "kimono" had been in use in France since 1876"[18]. Around these times the trend and longing for "things Japanese" in the West was mostly represented by the collection of Japanese prints, photography, handicrafts and souvenirs, purchased in Japan by foreign travelers and collectors or sold in Europe among artists. One of the motifs of these "things Japanese" were images of women clad in kimonos, which were normally associated with the world of the courtesans and *geishas*.

If kimonos were promoted in 1936 as the form of "Japanese Dress", the traveler to Japan would have found the kimono the type of cloth, worn in the provincial areas and in the cities by mostly women since most Japanese men were already wearing western fashions and uniforms for work from the beginning of the twentieth century. The image of kimono as "Japanese Dress" could be interpreted in the context of the publication of *Kawakatsu*, as consciously orientalized. Kimono as a commodity and women as wearers of its tradition were useful for the Japanese government and the tourist industry. They could manipulate this idea to symbolize the feminine and exotic Japan incarnated in the *geisha* icon, most likely with the intention of presenting Japan as a pleasurable tourist destiny for the western visitor, filling the West's craving for the exotic packed in kimono. Paradoxically, Tomiko Shimada writes in her essay on Changing Japan XX: Clothing Habits for the Japan Quarterly in 1962[19]:

"During the twenties and thirties, considerable inroads were made by Western clothing for women, especially with the adoption of schoolgirl's uniforms and Western clothes for working women"

However, Shimada also writes:

"All women of those times, even though they had spent their student's days in Western- style school uniforms, would revert to Japanese clothes after graduation and marriage"

After the end of the Second World War the kimono became a dress used mostly in formal occasions, as noted by Shimada, a New Year's Dress and

17 Milhaupt, Terry Satsuki, 2006. p.p.34.
18 Fukai Akiko, 2007, p.p. 52.
19 Shimada, Tomiko, 1962, p.p. 354.

western fashion was the up-to-date form of dress for the home and for everyday life, for both women and men in the cities and in the countryside. The traveler at the time of the Olympic Games in 1964 might have lacked the experience of seeing women in their Japanese clothing. As the historian Kenneth B. Pyle explains:

> "The invention of tradition is a key element of modern nationalism and is not unique to Japan. To promote nationalism the elites manipulate and rework ideas, institutions, and cultural symbols from the past to forge a nationalist ideology that will serve present purpose yet still resonate with basic values and sentiments on which the social system rests."[20]

In the text of Milhaupt on the facets of the kimonos as reflections of Japanese modernity, one can look at the history of the modern kimono, its textile design and the marketing strategies used to sell it as a very exiting one (especially between the time that followed the opening of Japan to the West and the pre-war years in the forties). It helps to explain the possible reasons why the kimono seems to be revitalized while recalling the memories of kimono modern history; especially the aesthetic and marketing strategies of the *Taisho* era (1912-1926). This period of kimono culture that had been ignored until recent times by most Japanese is distant to the image of pure traditionalism and conservatism of the national dress that kimono became after the World War II.

Taisho Romanticism

Which characteristics make the aesthetic of the *Taisho* period an era to be re-interpreted in the context of a contemporary kimono revival?
Taisho was an age of growth, economically and culturally:

> "Economical prosperous and culturally expansive, the Taisho era was a unique cultural period in which strong Western influence merged with Japanese traditional ways. It was a brief interlude, before xenophobic nationalism and militarism shut off access to the West.21"

During this time, some artists were openly mixing the older traditions and European avant-garde aesthetics, ideals and practices. *Taisho* was the era in which department stores developed from being dry goods stores or *gofukuten*. The first one *"Mitsukoshi"* used to collaborate with textile manufactures commissioning artists to design advertisements or illustrate magazines covers with images of "a decade defined by leisure and consumption"[22].

---

20 Pyle, Kenneth B, 1996, p.p.127.
21 Mochinaga Brando, Reiko p.p.12.
22 Sato, Barbara, p.p.27.

"Mitsukoshi played perhaps the key role in creating a seemingly organic connection between Western culture, fine art, mass media, consumerism, feminine identity, nostalgia, and nationalism"[23]

Some artists like *Takehisa Yumeji* that used to travel, work and study in the United States and in Europe were hired by *Mitsukoshi*. One of *Takehisa Yumeji's* recurrent themes were women's portraits. His portraits are considered to best represent the aesthetic and sensibility of the *Taisho* period in Japanese Art.

Hugo Munsterberg writes in his book, The Japanese Print: A Historical Guide on the work and life of *Takehisa Yumeji*:

"He worked in oils, watercolors, and book and magazine illustration, but he is today most admired for his prints, which enjoy a great vogue with present-day Japanese collectors who have nostalgia for the Taisho era (...) Yumeji based his work on Gauguin and art nouveau (...) His style, highly original (...) combines expressionistic distortion of form with bright colors. Especially striking are his close-up portraits, with their pale faces and elongated forms, and scenes of contemporary life in which the tension and anxiety of this time of rapid change are vividly reflected"

The image used most effectively to integrate these ideas of anxiety and the scenes of contemporary life was a type of modern "*bijin*" or (contemporary beautiful women)[24]. The modern "*bijin*" may have been a housewife, a café waitress, a professional women or a "Modern Girl" depending on the women created in the advertisements and the targeted consumers of the time, mostly females who were consuming the products of the department stores.

"Department stores' posters and textile manufacturers also promoted their products through seasonal tradeshows that for the first time featured ready-to-wear kimonos displayed on mannequins, each labeled as an "ideal type" of woman"[25]

In a new publication edited by Seigensha in 2007 that gives an overview on Japanese Fashion history by author Kazuo Jo, one can follow the trend of kimonos between the 1910s and 1920s."Kimonos in the Taisho mode" of the era termed "Taisho Romanticism"26 are represented with an illustration of a women clad in a kimono with a combination of the garment and hairstyle inspired under the aesthetic of the women represented in Yumejis art. Specifically in the reproduction of the colored Japanese print of Takehisa Yumeji from 1914 called

---

23 Brown, Kendall, p.p.54.
24 Brown, Kendall, p.p.49.
25 Milhaupt, Terry Satsuki, 2006, p.p. 37. Wada, 1998, p.p.8.
26 The spirit of euphoria and optimism ascribed to the Taisho period is often termed, nostalgically, "Taisho Romanticism". Mochinaga Brando, Reiko p.p.12.

"Minayota print shop at Gofuku-bashi street" the outfits worn by the women seen in (figure 3, first kimono design on the left)

is most likely the style of kimono of a cafe waitress. Yumeji's influence in the representation of the different types of women and the styles of the Taisho period seems to be one of the most important sources of inspiration for the designers and kimono coordinators of today's contemporary kimono revival. Books on his work are favored also among young Japanese girls interested in kimono or in the personality and work of this artist.

Kimonos for the masse

As previously mentioned, during the Taisho period (1912-1926), large trading companies, textile manufactures, and department stores worked together with artists and designers developing strategies of commercialism, using women's portraits in its advertisements, as argued by Kendall Brown
„Women were key in the process of modifying modernity, creating a hybrid culture where Japanese and Western elements met harmoniously"27

Barbara Sato cited cultural historian Wakamori Taroo who used the feature "Taishou mass culture" to distinguish Japan's interwar period as a period of massification. Commercialism and "mass" consumption seemed to increase during this period especially after World War I, argues Sato. In her opinion the end of the war "affirmed the sociohistorical context bolstering a consumer culture in Japan. With women as a significant coefficient, the war stimulated new patterns of consumption"28. Taisho was the era when women started to work outside of the home, in this way there was a challenge to produce popular kimono designs for working women that could match the changes taking place in the lifestyle of the cities. One of the strategies used to reach the goal of kimono design for the masses was to revive the design of traditional patterns in oversized dimensions, such as umbrellas, arrows and dragonflies or paper cranes or to integrate the designs from foreign countries like Mondrian-like rectangles and triangles or symmetrical Art Deco design29. With the introduction of new technological inventions from the West like the jacquard loom (imported to Japan in 1873) spinning machines (1866) and chemical dyes also brought to Japan around the same time, textile techniques such as kasuri30 Japanese ikat reached a high level in its production.

---

27 Brown, Kendall, 2004, p.p. 57.
28 Sato, Barbara, 2003, p.p.30.
29 Mochinaga Brando, Reiko, 1996, p.p. 13)
30 Kasuri, ikat: A method of creating a reserved pattern by tie-dyeing yarn before weaving. Stinchecum, Amanda,1984, p.p.221.

On the basis of the synthesis of technology, and the mixing of materials and techniques, a new popular silk fabric for kimonos was created known as Meisen. Meisen kimonos had bold designs and were less expensive to purchase, they became popular among most girls and middle class women in the cities and in the countryside. Meisen were used as day-to-day clothing, they were practical and resistant silk kimonos used by ordinary people. The style of the Taisho Meisen kimono is said to represent the popular ideas of the era: democratization, universal education and equality of rights for men and women from whom the popular phrase "Taisho Democracy"[31] came to be known. With the repetition of patterns in colorful colors and graphically oversized motives, this type of silk kimono design expressed the technological advances that were changing the cosmopolitan centers of Japanese cities. During the years of the end of the Taisho era and the beginning of the Showa period, a natural catastrophe accelerated the changes of the urban scenery of Tokyo. The city of Tokyo was rebuilt in a highly westernized way with western styles of buildings, cafes and department stores that became the environment of the "Modern Girls".

"Following the Great Earthquake, consumerism became a way of representing and judging the new urban-centered culture. In its most visible form, consumerism was incarnated in the media, popular music, and jazz. It was symbolized by the neon lights, the cafés and dance halls, Western fashions, and the bobbed hair of the modern girl"[32]

The Modern Girl

Between the 1920s and 1930s, the "Modern Girl" appeared as a phenomenon in Japanese history.

> "The late 20s and early 30s marked the rise of the ultra-fashionable and ever-controversial young women known as *moga* short for *modaan gaaru* (modern girl). Defined physically by their cropped hair, heavy makeup, and Western style of clothes, *moga* often worked and thus had some degree of socio-economic independence"
>
> "Culturally and politically, in the minds of conservatives at least, *moga* threatened the established norms of feminine deportment and undermined the social order, if not the whole of Japanese culture"[33]

For the "Modern Girl and her companion the Modern Boy" to walk around the shopping areas of Tokyo city center at *Ginza* was the most popular way to show off their Western outfits. During this period of Japanese history, young people could enter beer halls and cabarets for the first time, listen to jazz being played, drop by dance clubs, and catch plays at the theater. It was a time when

---

31 Mochinaga Brando, Reiko, 1996, p.p. 13.
32 Sato, Barbara, 2003, p.p.32.
33 Brown, Kendall, 2004, p.p. 58.

women projected a new desire for freedom and independence, demanding equality in political as well as social arenas. In this context of emancipation the Japanese history researcher Miriam Silverberg sees the Modern Girl as a militant[34] woman:

> "The "Modern Girl" stood as the vital symbol of overwhelming "modern" or non-Japanese change instigated by both women and men (...) She stood for change at a time when state authority was attempting to reestablish authority and stability".

The Modern Girl had the flexibility to be a "mannequin girl" in trendy western or kimono fashions or be the image of a poster for beer and other beverage advertisements. As Barbaro Sato writes, the "Modern Girl" was chosen by Shiseido to illustrate its latest cosmetics and toiletries[35]. She was part of Japan's trend towards consumerism, a major trend in the popular culture of the 1920s[36].

Is this perhaps the role that the young models of the *mook* "*Kimono at Kyoto*" play today? Are they asked to become "militants" of their own culture?

Can this revived "Modern Girl" clad in kimono become an archetype of kimono fashion? Is her image a means to identify kimono with the Orientalist stereotypes of Japanese feminine beauty and therefore with sweetness and cuteness? Or is she emancipated from the feminist ideas that had considered the kimono the symbol of oppression and submission of the feudal Japanese woman. Can she decide when and where and how she wants to use her national dress?

Conclusion

"*Taisho Romanticism*" as fusion culture of Western and Japanese aesthetics is inspiring contemporary kimono designers.

Designers are reviving the kimono while remembering the vitality of women of the *Taisho* era.

This new wave of kimono revival targets the young Japanese, boys and girls whose parents also grew up wearing western style of clothing in everyday life. These generations did not learn how to put on their ethnic cloth. The question is, if this revival can help them to re-construct and to re-discover traces of Japanese modernity for future generations or if in the other hand the embrace of the kimono as an alternative dress for everyday life could end up just being another trend of fashion.

The future of contemporary kimonos is still uncertain. The placement of a market for contemporary kimonos in Japan depends on the close interrelation of the Japanese tourist and textile industry, the active support of native fashion and

---

34 Silverberg, Miriam, 1991, p.p. 263.
35 Sato, Barbara, 2003, p.p. 7.
36 Sato, Barbara, 2003, p.p. 7.

textile designers, kimono manufacturers and brand names of fashion design, indigenous and foreign.

Its appearance at time of globalization may reflect anxiety, which is typical of the beginning of a new century, fear of loss of tradition and of identity.

Bibliography

Assmann, Stephanie. Between Tradition and Innovation: The Reinvention of the Kimono in Japanese Consumer Culture. Fashion Theory, Volume 12, Issue 3, 2008.

Assmann, Jan. Das kulturelle Gedächtnis: Schrift, Erinnerung und politische Identität in frühen Hochkulturen. München (Beck) 1997.

Brown KH, Minichiello S. Taishåo chic. Honolulu: Honolulu Academy of Arts; 2001.

Brown KH. Postcards, Commerce and Creativity. In: Morse AN, Rimer JT, Brown KH. Art of the Japanese postcard: the Leonard A. Lauder Collection at the Museum of Fine Arts, Boston. Aldershot: Lund Humphries; 2004.

Dalby LC. Kimono: fashioning culture. London: Vintage; 20011993.

Hobsbawm EJ, Ranger TO. The Invention of tradition. Cambridge [Cambridgeshire]: Cambridge University Press; 1983.

Kondo DK. About face. New York: Routledge; 1997.

Milhaupt, Terry Satsuki. Facets of the Kimono: Reflections of Japans Modernity. In: Trede M. Arts of Japan: The John C. Weber Collection. ; 2006.

Mochinaga R. Bright and Daring: Japanese Kimonos in the Taisho Mode. In: Bright & Daring Japanese Kimonos in the Taisho Mode from the Oka Nobutaka Collection of the Suzaka Classic Museum. Honolulu Academy of Arts. 1996.

Munsterberg H. The Japanese print: a historical guide. New York: Weatherhill; 1982.

Pyle KB. The making of modern Japan. Lexington, Mass: D.C. Heath; 1996.

Sato B. The new Japanese woman: modernity, media, and women in interwar Japan. Durham, N.C.; London: Duke University Press; 2003.

Shimada, Tomiko. Changing Japan XX: Clothing Habits. Japan quarterly; 1962.

Silverberg, Miriam. The Modern Girl as a Militant. In: Bernstein GL. Recreating Japanese women, 1600-1945. Berkeley: University of California Press; 1991.

Stinchecum AM, Richard NN, Paul M. Kosode, 16th-19th century textiles from the Nomura Collection. New York: Japan Society; 1984.

Fukai Akiko. The Kimono and Parisian Mode. In: Van Assche A, Ember S. Fashioning kimono. Alexandria, Va: Art Services International; 2007.

Figure 1. taken from the Frontpiece of the mook "Kimono At Kyoto". Edited and printed in japan in year 2005 by Mitsumura Suiko Shoin.

Figure 2. Photo by Oly Firsching-Tovar. Kyoto October 2008.

Figure 3. Taken from the book "Japanese Fashion", edited and printed in Japan by Segensha in year 2007, p. 36-37.

Bollywood, ou la réinvention de l'orientalisme et de l'occidentalisme dans le cinéma indien actuel

Daniel Devoucoux

L'Orient n'existe plus, il n'a jamais existé, c'est un rêve de l'occident, prétend le cinéaste Volker Schlöndorff.[1] S'il subsiste pourtant une vision idéalisée de l'orient, c'est bel et bien dans le cinéma occidental. Celui-ci est même l'inventeur de l'orientalisme à grand spectacle moderne qui l'alimente depuis sa naissance.

Les théories de l'exotisme - version orient – ont longtemps eu pour unique perspective le regard occidental sur les cultures asiatiques et arabes. Cette optique unidimensionnelle est contredite aujourd'hui par nombre de cinémas asiatiques, à commencer par celui de Bollywood. Car Bollywood n'est plus objet d'observation exotique mais est devenu sujet conquérant. Pour palier à la crise du cinéma des années 1990 et la perte d'une clientèle aisée[2], Bollywood adopte alors diverses stratégies.

Counter-Orientalism au cinéma

La conception de self-, revers ou counter-orientalism présuppose le regard local et le public autochtone au centre de la mise en scène et de l'image d'identité indienne que tente de transmettre Bollywood.[3] Il ne cherche en aucun cas à servir au public occidental les images exotiquement colorées et l'ambiance dynamique que cherche ce public.

Le fait que l'industrie cinématographique bollywoodienne ait depuis longtemps intégré nombre de formes de divertissement d'origine occidentale, qu'elle refaçonne, n'est cependant pas étrangère aux effets self-orientalistes. Ceux-ci sont en effet liés aux techniques et aux processus de stylisation et de typification des personnages, des caractères, des ambiances, des situations, des espaces et bien sûr des costumes utilisés aussi bien par Hollywood que par Bollywood. Le cinéma indien les oriente cependant dans son sens, c'est à dire à partir d'une sémiotique – et les processus de connotations et dénotations qui la soutiennent – consensuelle, opérante dans les différents cinémas indiens et basée

---

1 Le Faussaire / Die Fälschung (1981). Ce texte recoupe et prolonge celui écrit en allemand: Daniel Devoucoux: Historizität und Modernität: Kostümstrategien in Bollywood-Filmen seit den 1990er Jahren. In: Susanne Marschall (Hg.): Indiens Kino-Kulturen. Geschichte – Dramaturgie – Ästhetik, Marburg, Schüren 2013.
2 India Today Vol XXVI, n° 1/2000 (Janvier), p. 20-26; Vol. XXVI, n° 4/2001, p.24-30;
3 C'est une des thèses de Wilhelm Halnfass transposée au cinéma : Voir Eli Franco / Karin Preisedanz (ed): Beyond Orientalism. The Work of Wilhelm Halbfass and its Impact in India. Rodopi, Amsterdam 1997, p. 16.

sur des contextes culturels variés mais grosso-modo connus de l'ensemble du monde indien.

Bollywood n'est en aucun cas un miroir passif des relations existantes mais au contraire une structure médiatique puissante qui légitime ou discrédite certaines formes d'interactions. Prenant de plus en plus en considération le public nanti des *Non Residents Indians* (NRI), en particulier celui installé en Europe – plus particulièrement en Grande Bretagne - et aux Etats-Unis, ils jouent souvent sur les images nostalgiques stéréotypés, rejoignant ici paradoxalement l'imagerie occidentale sur l'Orient. Ce n'est donc pas par hasard non plus si le public occidental y voit malgré tout ce qu'il voulait voir.

Je décrierai donc ici par le terme self-orientalism un processus orienté vers l'intérieur d'adoption d'images extrêmement connotées, voire coloniales dans un contexte global nouveau poursuivant d'autres buts et intentions à travers des stratégies très variées, en particulier celles étant à même de créer des effets d'attraction forte.[4]

Ce concept de self-orientalism ne se réfère donc pas fondamentalement à l'Ouest. Dorine Kondo par exemple dans son ouvrage sur les designers japonais contemporains parle de «counter-orientalism» pour désigner une méthode critique qui questionne l'identité japonaise à travers les stéréotypes asiatiques, en particulier chinois.[5] D'autres comme Sandra Niessen voient dans le self-orientalisme une conséquence de la globalisation actuelle, surtout dans le domaine de la consommation et de la mode, par laquelle d'anciennes images et valeurs sont ravivées et mises au goût du jour de manière souterraine comme par exemple l'image de la femme asiatique soumise et consommatrice passive.[6] Même chose pour Mita Banerjee qui soulève les dessous de la relation entre la haute couture de Issey Miyake et l'utilisation qui en est faite dans le cinéma hindi.[7]

En réalité, ces images orientalistes sont sapées et détournées subtilement par les intéressées en de nouvelles formes de pratiques et d'images de soi. Les conséquences en sont si nombreuses qu'elles ne sauraient ici être comprimées en un bref résumé.[8]

---

4 Voir à ce sujet par exemple l'article de Syed Farid Alatas : The Meaning of Alternatives Discourses. In : Srilata Ravi (ed.), Asia in Europe, Europe in Asia. Institute of Southeast Asian Studies, Singapour 2004, p. 57-78.
5 Dorin Kondo: About face. Performing Race in Fashion and Theater, New York 1997, p. 55-58.
6 Voir. Sandra Niessen / Ann Maire Leskovich / Carla Jones (Hg.), Re-Orienting Fashion.. The Globalization of Asian Dress, Oxford et New York 2003, p. 8-17.
7 Mita Banerjee: Bollywood meets Issey Miyake. Indo Chic versus Asian fusion fashion in contemporary hindi-cinema. Lisa Lau / Cristina Ann (ed.): Re-Orientalism NS SOUTH Asian Identity Politics. Routledge, Londres 2011, p. 124-133.
8 Voir à ce sujet Emma Tarlo: Clothing Matters. Cloth and Identity in India. Londres 1996, p. 33-42.

L'âge global nous oblige à réviser complètement nos idées et nos images, y compris en matière vestimentaire. L'analyse des films, même à caractère anti-coloniaux comme *Lagaan*, ne peut donc plus être la même qu'au XXè siècle. S'il reste vrai que le chemin menant de l'ouest à l'est – avec son sanglant sillage colonialiste - n'est absolument pas le même que celui qui conduit de l'est à l'ouest, la logique globale économique et consommatrice fait cependant de plus en plus abstraction de ces différences historiques lourdes de conséquences.

Le revers-orientalisme ne « se réfère à aucune forme artistique particulière, mais à toute représentation emphatique sur les costumes locaux »[9], les formes, les manières et ambiances locales qui possèdent une force de fascination esthétique voire même souvent une charge érotique particulière. Le revers-orientalisme n'est plus un « autre » en relation à l'ouest mais il est devenu quelque chose d'hybride, s'appuyant sur des processus différenciés.

Le „regard touriste"

A la source du boom self-orientaliste / occidentaliste actuel, il faut plutôt voir la conséquence de ce que John Urry appelle *le regard touriste* (*The Tourist Gaze* est ici un terminus technicus, un concept de recherche) qui guide aujourd'hui la recherche d'images exotiques, dépaysantes ou provoquant simplement même un certain «Thrill».[10]

Ce régime du regard inclut et mêle aussi bien le tourisme lui-même et la publicité que le cinéma, la presse, la télévision, la mode et le design, le théâtre et l'opéra, la littérature et l'internet. L'interaction mutuelle et étroite des médias et leur influence réciproque les uns sur les autres multiplient les effets de résonance et peuvent être considérés comme des éléments décisifs conduisant à cette omniprésence du «regard touristique». Ce processus d'interconnexion est également à l'origine du phénomène étonnant qui fait que d'un côté aujourd'hui chacun devient touriste dans sa propre ville, d'un autre qu'on se sente au cinéma chez soi.

Ce régime du regard s'ancre certes à des conceptions historiquement forgées mais pour les déplacer ou les réinventer par des moyens nouveaux, changeant d'autant leurs significations et leur impact. Cela ne retire pas leur caractère stylisant et stéréotypant, mais le détourne.

Cet aspect interactif peut être illustré de plusieurs façons. Chaque année, toujours plus de touristes occidentaux se rendent à Mumbay pour essayer d'y entrevoir les idoles de Bollywood.[11] La branche touristique a compris très vite le

---

9 Sandra Ponzansci: Beyond the Black Venus. Colonial Sexual Politics and Contemporary Visual Pratices, p. 167.
10 Des critères précis définissent le regime de ce regard. John Urry: The Tourist Gaze, Sage Publications, Thosand Oaks/Californie et Londres 2002 (Seconde Edition), p. 1-15.
11 Toutes ces remarques, comme celles plus générales sur le cinéma sont certes le résultat de plusieurs voyages dans le cadre de recherches universitaires en Inde, mais n'importe quel voyageurs peut en faire l'expérience.

profit qu'elle pouvait tirer de ce nouvel engouement et de nombreuses agences à Mumbai se sont spécialisés dans le tour des endroits où habitent les grands noms du cinéma bollywoodien, à Juhu, à Bandra, Malabar Hill, Andheri ou à Versova. La maison de Shah Rukh Khan et de sa femme Gauri, un long bungalow classé monument historique, présente à elle seule un attrait quasi magnétique.

En même temps un flot toujours plus nombreux de touristes Indiens issus des couches fortunées et provenant de toute l'Inde se rend en Suisse, en Autriche, en Afrique du Sud, en Nouvelle Zélande, à Londres ou à New York pour y retrouver l'endroit où les films ou bien certaines scènes mémorables de films ont été tournés.

Le caractère, le régime du regard est central pour les stratégies de l'industrie touristique[12] et j'ajouterai pour la grosse industrie cinématographique également. Dean MacCannell et John Urry insistent sur le fait qu'à la différence des pèlerins, qui concentrent leur intérêt avec modestie et respect sur un lieu sacré unique, le regard touristique connaît lui au contraire de nombreux centres d'intérêt.[13] Dans le cas de Bollywood, je mêlerai cependant ici les deux perspectives.

Ainsi l'endroit de New York sur les rives de l'Hudson près du Brooklyn Bridge où Amman (Shah Rukh Khan) avoue enfin à Naina (Preity Zinta) sa passion sans espoir dans le film *Kal Ho Naa Ho* (2003, Fig. 3) est devenu un véritable lieu de pèlerinage. Des artistes l'ont même pris comme modèle et les Indiens l'appellent depuis le Kal Ho Naa Ho Bridge (oder KHNH-Bridge).[14]

Cela suppose que l'œil voit en ces lieux des signes relationnels qui renvoient aux films, aux acteurs, aux chants, aux danses et aux costumes. Pour Kal Ho Naa Ho par exemple, ce sont deux silhouettes lointaines prises en plongée, l'une droite, l'autre penchée, dont on ne reconnaît justement que les costumes, un Sweat-Shirt en sueur et un jean à pinces pour l'un, une longue robe noire moulant le corps pour l'autre. La perspective est reprise trois fois dans le film, chaque fois en la déplaçant légèrement: le choc émotionnel est garanti.

Ce qui rapproche donc pèlerins et touristes, c'est l'expérience du lieu, la différence entre le quotidien, le familier et l'insolite, l'exceptionnel. Le regard touristique est un regard sémiotique et les touristes sont tous des sémiotistes qui partout voient les signes qu'ils y mettent. Ils sont, comme certains scientifiques, des fanatiques du signe.

---

12 Urry 2002, op. cit., p. 12-13.
13 D. MacCannell: The Tourist, Schocken, New York 1999, p. 58; Urry 2002, op. cit.., p. 10.
14 Même chose pour Berlin où suite au tournage de certaines scenes de "Don 2", une carte et un site électronique ont été mis à disposition du public pour lui permettre de suivre les traces de Shah Rukh Khan à travers Berlin, du stade olympique à la East Side Gallery en passant par Alexanderplatz, l'opéra, la salle des concerts sur le Gendarmenmarkt, etc.
Voir http://www.visitberlin.de/sites/default/files/don2_city_map.pdf.

C. Campbell et J. Urry mettent étroitement en rapport l'essor du régime de regard touristique et la consommation moderne.[15] «Il y a une dialectique de la nouveauté et de l'insatiabilité au cœur du consumérisme moderne»[16], tout comme au cœur de la mode et à celui du cinéma.

Quand ils entreprennent un voyage en Suisse, en Autriche ou en Bavière, les indiens aisés «savent reconnaître chaque montagne de leurs films et achètent sur place même ensuite les costumes faisant partie de ce paysage: costumes de dirndl, culottes de cuir, chapeaux feutrés à plume, etc ».[17] Ce sont ces costumes qui donnent au lieu une couleur et intensité visuelle propre. L'appropriation des costumes autochtones devient là une opération rituelle quasi magique.

L'occidentalisme de Bollywood

Un autre aspect des films de Bollywood – j'aborde ici le second point - est l'occidentalisme forcéné dont il fait preuve ces dernières années. Le terme «occidentalisme» renvoie aux travaux du philosophe égyptien Hassan Hanafi qui provoqua à la sortie de son livre de violentes discussions.[18] Mais ce terme échappe lui aussi de plus en plus à son inventeur et à sa définition.

On peut le comprendre ici comme une manière particulière moins d'appréhender et de comprendre que de redéfinir l'occident d'après des éléments de culture soigneusement choisis comme la mode, les styles de vie ou les gadgets techniques par exemple.

Ce qui caractérise l'occidentalisme indien au cinéma, c'est que, au-delà des formes et des images, la perception des cultures locales réelles est pratiquement nulle ou au régime le plus bas.[19] Nous le savons pour le cinéma européen ou américain depuis l'époque coloniale (donc la naissance du cinéma), mais c'est également valable d'une certaine manière pour le cinéma bollywoodien. Celui-ci fait d'ailleurs souvent preuve, dans le contenu de ses films, d'un extraordinaire

---

15 Colin Campbell: The Romantic Ethic and the Spirit of Modern Consumerism, Basil Blackwell, Oxford 1987, op. cit., p. 88-95.

16 J. Urry 2002, op. cit., p. 13. Urry insiste également sur le rôle de ce qu'il appelle l'industrie du patrimoine (p. 94-102) et sur celui de la photographie (p. 127-129)

17 Der Spiegel 4.8.2006: Von Bombay nach Bayernwood..

18 Hassan Hanafi: Introduction à la science de l'occidentalisme, Le Caire 1992. La japonologue Hijiya Kirschnereit en résume ainsi la quintessence: Lorsque l'Est sera capable de voir dans l'ouest un objet de connaissance et non plus une source de savoir, alors il se libérera de sa domination intellectuelle. Dans cette étude critique Kirschnereit montre pourtant que cette catégorie admet dans les pays asiatiques de multiples utilisations et ne s'entend pratiquement jamais comme élément complémentaire ou comme contrepoids au terme Orientalisme de Said. Le Japon l'utilise par exemple comme concept historique et culturel de démarcation par rapport à la Chine. Irmela Hijiya-Kirschnereit : Okzidentalismus. Eine Problemskizze. In: Naguschewski, Dirk / Trabant, Jürgen (ed.): Was heißt hier „fremd". Adademie, Berlin 1997, p. 243-251.

19 Même le film My Name is Khan de Karan Johar ne fait que quelques faibles concessions au public occidental.

nationalisme culturel et prend même en s'élargissant des allures impériales, en Inde d'abord.

Par le cinéma de Bollywood en effet presque tous les indiens, nous dit l'écrivain Suketu Mehta, même s'ils n'y sont jamais allés, «sont devenus des habitants de Bombay» et reconnaissent tout de suite «la large courbe de Marine Drive, la plage de Juhu, la porte de l'ouest – c'est ainsi qu'on nomme l'aéroport d'Andhéri», tous à Dehra Dun, à Jaipur, «à Kanpur comme dans le Kerala».[20]

A l'ouest ensuite, car même lorsque l'action des films se situent à Londres, en Suisse ou au cœur de New York[21], la culture locale, anglaise, suisse ou américaine, est superbement ignorée, dans la meilleure tradition de l'expression exotique. Elle n'entre pratiquement pas, sinon comme décor, dans l'histoire et ses valeurs ne jouent absolument aucun rôle dans le film. La seule chose que Bollywood prend en considération, se sont les formes de l'occident, de l'architecture, des styles de vie et surtout de la mode et des costumes tels que Bollywood les voient. Cela vaut pour *Kal Ho Naa Ho* comme pour *My Name is Khan*, dont la campagne publicitaire fut lancée de manière inattendue à l'aér$oport de Newark (New Jersey) au mois d'août 2009[22].

L'occident ne remplit plus aujourd'hui pour Bollywood le rôle d'un lieu de punition mais il reste encore majoritairement un horizon d'exil. La mode occidentale, elle par contre, n'a plus rien d'un signe de décadence. Non plus seulement les costumes, mais les occidentaux eux-mêmes amènent maintenant une note exotique dans les films de Bollywood. En fin de compte, Bollywood est tout comme le cinéma américain, dont il ne suit heureusement pas les genres narratifs, toujours à lire à la fois dans le sens du poil et à rebrousse-poil.

La mode et la consommation sont devenues une sorte de passeport de la modernité, à la fois symbole et instrument, pour les classes moyennes indiennes.[23] C'est pourquoi, l'orientation d'une grande partie de la production bollywoodienne vers ces couches moyennes prodigues, dont les figures de proue sont sans conteste les acteurs Shah Rukh Khan et Aamir Khan, change radicalement le look des films.

---

20 Suketu Mehta, op. cit., p. 500.
21 Comme dans les Blockbuster Dilwale Dulhania Le Jayenge (DDLJ) ou dans Kabhi Alvida Naa Kehna) (KANK),
22 Grâce aux douaniers américains de l'aéroport de Newark (New Jersey) qui ont retenu pendant plus d'une heure la vedette du film, Shah Rukh Khan, à cause de son nom pour «inspection de routine» en août 2009. Cette mesure, semblant illustrer le film qui thématise les préjugés auxquels sont confrontés les indiens musulmans d'Amérique depuis le 11 septembre 2001, a été largement commentée par la presse «occidentale» mais plus copieusement encore par celle de la quasi-totalité des pays africains et asiatiques.
23 Pavan K. Varma: The Geat Indian Middle Class, La Nouvelle Delhi, Londres et New York 1998, p. 156.

Rappel bref

Cela commença dès les années 1990 avec par exemple le film *DDLJ* (*Dilwale Dulhania Le Jayenge/Jaège* 1995, de Aditya Chopra), le plus grand succès de toute l'histoire du cinéma indien (avant *Ghajini* et *3 idiots* dernièrement), dans lequel on voit même Shah Rukh Khan à la gare de Saanen (dans le canton de Bern) affublé d'un chapeau tyrolien.

Dans le courant des années 1990, on assiste donc pour la première fois à une véritable césure dans le cinéma hindi ou indoustani. «Ce qui plait à l'ingénieur IT de San José», écrit Suketu Mehta, «n'est plus ce qui intéresse également le paysan du Bilaspur. Des cinéastes comme Yash Chopra, Subhaish Ghai, Mani Ratnam ou Karan Johar changent alors le contenu de leurs films pour l'aligner plus sur le goût des indiens de l'étranger (NRI: Non Resident Indian), de qui à long terme, on pouvait tirer plus d'argent». Tanuja, cité plus haut, en résumant les intentions des cinéastes d'exclure la pauvreté pour s'orienter sur des critères exclusifs de « beauté » donnait le ton pour deux décennies.[24]

Par voie de conséquence les costumes et les décors des films pour le marché global (comme *Kuch Kuch Hota Hai*, *Lagaan*, *Devdas* ou *Rang de Basanti*) deviennent plus élaborés. En même temps on s'oriente de plus en plus vers les costumes occidentaux.[25]

C'est ainsi qu'avant le tournage de son film *Kuch Kuch Hota Hai* (1998), nous racontent Anupama Chopra, le cinéaste Karan Johar entreprit avec son ami le créateur de costume Manish Malhotra plusieurs voyages à Londres pour y rechercher des costumes et des tissus qui conviendraient au film.[26]

Dans *Kuch Kuch Hota Hai* - et de nombreux films qui vont suivre -, le fétichisme des marques vestimentaires occidentales prend non seulement une valeur symbolique mais aussi, pour reprendre Balasescu, quasiment érotique, remplaçant celle de la peau.[27]

Pour être sûr que le public reconnaisse bien toute la peine et les moyens déployées «Karan et Manish choisirent sciemment des costumes où l'on voyaient clairement qu'ils provenaient de créateurs de mode étrangers: beaucoup portait un logo en travers de la poitrine. Dans la première scène où ils jouent ensemble Anjali (joué par Kajol) porte un survêtement de basketball marqué DKNY, Rahul (Shah Rukh Khan), lui, y préfère le polo et les vêtements de sport Gap».[28]

---

24 S. Mehta, op. cit., p. 502.
25 Depuis que l'ouest dans les années 1990 «avec ses promesses séduisantes de modernité, de glamour et un style de vie coûteux avait fait son entrée dans les foyers des couches moyennes indiennes». Anupama Chopra, op. cit., p. 24.
26 A. Chopra, ibid., S. 202.
27 Balasescu, op. cit., p. 100.
28 A. Chopra, op. cit., S. 202-203. Cette sensibilité générale du nouveau Bollywood peut expliquer l'attitude réticente de l'acteur Amitabh Bachchan (une véritable légende du cinéma indien), vis à vis du film Slumdog Millionaire, qui bien que tourné par un metteur en scène

Plus loin ce sont des anoraks Tommy Hilfiger, des sweat-shirts Levi ou Speedo, à une époque donc où la confection de masse et les copies de ces marques n'avaient pas encore inondé le marché indien (Fig. 4). Cela en serait plutôt la conséquence. Les cinéastes de la diaspora avec leur cinéma des deux cultures (*Kick it like Beckham*) et surtout le public des Non Residents Indiens ne sont bien sûr pas étrangers à ce développement de l'occidentalisme dans les films de Bollywood.

Dans les états de Bihar, de l'Orissa ou d'Uttar Pradesh par contre, il existe encore un plaisir à entendre des histoires, ici les villageois regardent encore la Ramilila, dit Suketu Mehta, une version théatrale du Ramayana. Le cinéma doit donc prendre en considération ces différences. Les films Hindi peuvent unir Bihar et Delhi, même Bihar et Karachi, mais certainement pas Bihar et Londres, résume Mehta.[29]

Tout comme pour l'orientalisme, il existe aussi une dimension érotique de l'exotisme occidentaliste indien, qui se commercialise avec succès. La brusque vague des mini- et micro-jupes dans les films de Bollywood des années 1990 jusqu'à aujourd'hui – qu'on chercherait en vain dans les rues de Chennai, Kolkata ou Dehli (2009) - est à comprendre en ce sens. Il faudrait s'attarder plus sur les territoires du genre (gender) dans ce cinéma de Bollywood, et le relire de cette perspective (ce que font nombre d'études et de critiques indiennes). Les rapports entre sexes sont une clé essentielle pour comprendre une société perdue entre les images du passé (Khajuraho) la récusation du sexe par Gandhi, le manque de normes sociales qui permettrait plus d'ouverture entre les sexes, l'expérience dramatique des femmes liées au divorce ou à la situation de veuve, les images globales de MTV, celles de Bollywood et le poids du néo-libéralisme économique.

Rares sont les œuvres qui timidement comme dans *Swades* (2004 de Gowariker) ou frontalement comme dans *Bandit Queen* (1994 de Shekar Kappur), *Fire* (1996 de Deepa Mehta) ou *Satta* (2003 de Madhur Bhandarkar), abordent la thématique du genre (Gender).

Dans des films comme *Maqbool* (2003) ou *Black* (2005), qui sortent der ce que l'on connaît de Bollywood, puisque qu'il n'y a aucune scène de chants et de

---

anglais est considéré (oscar oblige) comme un film indien. Interview BBC-Asia. JuIIIet 2009. Cette position n'est pas nouvelle. En 1957 déjà la déesse de l'écran Rakha (Mother India) avait invectivé les metteurs en scène comme Satyajit Ray, Ritwik Ghatak, Mrinal Sen et le „New Indian Cinema" avec l'argument qu'il ne montraient que la pauvreté de l'Inde et les petites gens.

29 S. Mehta, op. cit., p. 503. Il raconte l'histoire suivante: «Un jour de 1998, je me retrouvais dans une région isolée de l'état d'Arunchal Pradesh, dont l'accès, même pour les résidents indiens, exigeait une autorisation spéciale. A un petit comptoir qui distribuait du thé, sur une route de campagne, une femme m'informa sur les lieux sacrés du coin: Et ici, près du château d'eau du village, on a tourné `Koyla´. Shah Rukh Khan est venu ici. Les dieux de Bombay ont remplacé les anciens dieux tribaux». (traduction de l'auteur), ibid, p. 504.

danse, les costumes – eux aussi la plupart du temps occidentaux - jouent un rôle plus subtil et montrent que Bollywood possède plus d'une corde qualitative à son arc. «Black» par exemple est un film qui raconte l'histoire d'une aveugle muette et sourde (joué par Rani Mukherjee) et de son éducateur (Amitabh Bachchan). Ce film n'a pourtant rien de triste ou de mélancolique. Même si les costumes sont noirs ou sombres, c'est un film plein de joie de vivre et de couleurs. Pas les couleurs que nous avons l'habitude de voir, «mais de celles qu'on apprend à voir», nous dit le metteur en scène Sanjay Leela Bhansali. C'est un film sur la beauté intérieure des gens et des choses. *Maqbool*, de Vishal Bhardwaj, une transposition moderne de Macbeth en milieu gangster, joue encore plus en finesse dans le détail des costumes comme dans le scénario et l'esthétique, presque en dehors des normes de Bollywood.

Un film-bilan: *Om Shanti Om*

Les derniers films de Farah Khan comme *Main Hoon Na*, une histoire où se mêlent romantisme de terminal bon teint et terrorisme, et surtout *Om Shanti Om* (2007) nous offrent une sorte de bilan provisoire de Bollywood, en particulier en ce qui concerne les costumes, dans la mesure où le look des personnages et les scènes d'action participent activement au style de ces films.

Farah Khan fait partie du groupe de cinéastes qui ont le plus influencé Bollywood ces dernières années, en particulier en matière de costumes. Dans *Om Shanti Om*, de l'aveu même de la cinéaste, les couleurs des costumes et des décors jouent un rôle central et suivent le motif des quatre éléments, la terre, l'eau, le vent et le feu.[30]

Les costumes soutiennent de plus la constitution des espaces, c'est-à-dire dans le film des espaces clos, puisque le film a essentiellement été tourné en studios.[31] Alexandra Schneider a souligné que les espaces dans le cinéma hindi sont des espaces imaginaires qui suivent d'autres règles que celles du cinéma occidental.[32] On comprendra donc bien la place qu'occupent les costumes dans l'agencement d'un tel espace imaginaire.

Dans la mesure où l'action est supposée se dérouler pendant les années 1970 et aujourd'hui, le film se replie sur un certain nombre de clichés pour restituer ces époques et marquer leur différence. Pour ce faire, il joue au maximum sur la mode occidentaliste.

Il n'empêche, ces costumes sont grandioses et lorsque sur l'air romantique *Aankohn Mein Teri*, Om (Shah Rukh Khan encore) dans sa veste rouge et noire à gros carreaux reste accroché à son idole et se met à la suivre, le public indien

---

30 Interview Farah Khan. In: Bonus du film Om Shanti om.
31 Dans les Film City, Goregon, les Filmistan Studio et les Yash Raj Studios à Mumbay.
32 Sur les traces du poète Javed Akhtar. Alexandra Schneider: Im Niemandland von Affekt und Aspiration. In: Susanne Marschall (Hg.), Indien. Film-Konzepte 3, München 2006, p. 39-40.

est aux anges et nous avec (Fig. 5). Ce sont de brefs moments où le cinéma commercial parvient à devenir magique.

Le film par ses citations sans fin[33] - également ses citations vestimentaires - fait appel à la culture cinématographique phénoménale que possède tout spectateur indien, illustrée également par l'apparition brève de 31 grandes stars du cinéma indien. On y trouve même la fameuse pose saraswati des danseuses. C'est en même temps Bollywood qui se parodie et un hommage au cinéma: un métafilm.

Si l'on observe bien ces deux films, on s'aperçoit qu'ils n'exclut pourtant jamais les costumes indiens qui reviennent souvent, surtout dans les scènes de chant et de danse. Cela est valable pour pratiquement tous les films actuels de Bollywood, même si les films sont tournés entièrement à New York, on y trouve parfois des costumes adivasi.[34]

L'occidentalisme n'est donc pas ici à comprendre comme un retournement du phénomène Orientaliste ou comme contre-stratégie à celui-ci, mais comme le résultat de nombreux processus qui s'interfèrent, offrant des options supplémentaires. Il s'éloigne donc fortement d'un concept symétrique à celui d'Edward Said[35], mais il est sans aucun doute une réponse aux défis engendrés par «l'ouest».

Les vêtements occidentaux dans le cinéma indien ne sont pas nouveaux, puisqu'on les trouve dès le début du cinéma. Ils n'ont pourtant de décennies en décennies, pas la même signification. Dans les années 1960 et 70 justement, ce sont surtout les méchants qui s'habillaient à l'occidental, et ils le font encore quelquefois aujourd'hui. Dans les années 1980 ils étaient signe de décadence. Cet occidentalisme vestimentaire devient aujourd'hui paradoxalement un aspect du nationalisme culturel omniprésent de Bollywood. Que s'est-il donc passé?

---

33 De films Indiens d'abord puisque les acteurs actuels – grâce à la technique – interviennent même dans des extraits de films anciens comme Karz (1980) de Subhash Gai. Sharukh Khan est affublé des costumes de Rishi Kapoor, qui jouait dans ce film, pour la chanson Dhoom Tanaa et Depita Padukone se retrouve aux côtés de Sunil Dutt, dans Amrapali (1966) ou à ceux de Jeetendra dans Jay – Vejay 2 (1977) et Humjoli (1970). Films américains ensuite avec des films comme Chantons sous la pluie (1952) de Stanley Donen et Gene Kelly ou Suzie et les Bäcker Boys (1989) de Steven Kloves avec Jeff Bridge et Michelle Pfeiffer et même Autant en emporte le vent (1939) de Victor Fleming.
34 Noms que se sont donnés les minorités aborigènes de l'Inde (environ 8% de la population), ainsi les Dhils du Gujarat et du Madhya Pradesh, les Mundaris du Jharkhand et de l'Orissa, les Santalis du Bengale occidental, les Gonds (Koitur), une population Adivasi nombreuse, repartie sur le pays ou les Nagas du Nord-Est. Voir à ce sujet Madhusree Mukerjee : The Land of naked peoples. Encounters with Stone Age Islanders. Pinguin Books, Delhi 2003.
35 I. Huiya Kirschnereit; op. cit., S. 154-159.

Transfert?

«L'Inde a toujours eu un grand appétit pour les influences extérieures qu'elle absorbait», dit la cinéaste Mira Nair. Dans ce contexte, il est normal, que les gens non seulement parlent anglais, hindi et punjabi (*Monsoom Wedding*) «mais qu'une jeune femme porte le matin une jupe-mini et le soir un sari».[36] Le concept de transfert, si souvent utilisé dans ce cas, est-il apte à décrire les interactions complexes qui se jouent ici ?[37] Il serait en effet tout à fait erroné de croire qu'avec les vêtements de l'ouest, le cinéma indien en reprend aussi les valeurs.

Si l'on veut le garder le terme il est donc préférable de définir le type de relation en jeu, car «les attitudes vestimentaires sont une arène dans laquelle sont négociés les conflits individuels et culturels engendré par la modernité», écrit l'anthropologue Gabriele Mentges. « Cela a entre autre pour conséquence que la mode transférée dans d'autres contextes génère d'autres significations. Dans la mesure où avec la mode sont également thématisés de nouvelles images du corps et des sexes, les conflits culturels sont préprogrammés et particulièrement virulents».[38]

Bollywood simplifie le monde vestimentaire. La variété et la multiplicité des costumes indiens sont synthétisées par le cinéma de Mumbay en une gamme relativement restreinte de formes et motifs - mais pas de couleurs -, qui sont supposés valoir comme dénominateur commun pour la totalité de l'Inde. Le large éventail des saris et des dhotis par exemple est réduit à une toute petite palette pendant que les vêtements occidentaux bollywoodisés occupent de plus en plus d'espace.

Ce serait peine perdue de chercher dans l'Inde des années 1990 et même d'aujourd'hui un collège où les étudiants s'habillent comme dans *Kuch Kuch Hota Hai* (Abb. 6) ou dans *Main Hoon Na*. Ce que voulaient Karan Johar et Farah Khan, les metteurs en scène de chacun de ces films, c'était d'abord créer de nouveaux standards stylistiques dans le cinéma indien.

De nombreux tabous vestimentaire qui n'ont depuis longtemps plus cours dans les films occupent toujours le devant de la scène sociale. Montrer ses jambes pour une femme exige une connaissance profonde de l'endroit où elle se trouve. Si cela est possible dans certains quartiers, dans les réceptions à Mumbai ou dans les cafés des classes moyennes de Bengalore, cela l'est moins dans les

---

36 Interview mit Mira Nair. Der Spiegel 5.10.2002.
37 Issu de la psychanalyse, le concept de transfert est aujourd'hui usuel dans les sciences sociales et humaines ainsi que dans celles de la communication, non plus dans le sens de projection mais comme technique de propagation et d'annexion. Sur le cheminement du terme, voir l'ouvrage collectif dirigé par Martine Bercot et Michel Erman (ed.) : Transferts de concepts : d'un savoir à l'autre, Presses Universitaires de Dijon, Dijon 2006.
38 Gabriele Mentges: Massgeschneiderte Identität. (Titre original de l'auteur: Indian Fashion – Fashion in India). In: Zeitschrift für KulturAustausch 4/2002 (traduction de l'auteur), p. 52-55, ici p. 54.

grandes villes du Rajasthan, ce que les visiteurs occidentaux ne semblent pas toujours comprendre, et cela devient quasiment dangereux dans certaines villes du Bihar ou de l'Uttar Pradesh.

D'un autre côté, et pour paraphraser Paul Rabinow[39], les images sont aussi des faits sociaux et l'influence de Bollywood n'est pas étrangère à la propagation de cette mode occidentale, ni au fait que dans les grands centres urbains le sari perd de plus en plus son rôle de symbole de la femme hindoue orthodoxe ou le Shalwar Kameez celui de vêtement musulman.

Tous deux sont devenus des options de mode, tout comme l'est la mode occidentale, parmi d'autres qui définissent non plus des statuts familiaux, hiérarchiques ou religieux mais de plus en plus des goûts de consommateur. Il n'empêche, la rupture qui sépare les couches moyennes du reste de la population, soit les ¾ de l'Inde, en particulier celle des campagnes, est plus profonde que jamais et elle se traduit aussi par les vêtements.

Il faut finalement comprendre ici le self-orientalisme et l'occidentalisme de Bollywood comme des techniques d'attraction parmi d'autres, au même titre que les effets spéciaux ou le sound-track: Bollywood est essentiellement un cinéma d'attraction, au sens des sciences des médias. Ce regard bollywoodien est également un miroir du régime de vision consensuel indien et sud-asiatique avec leur ambivalence mais aussi leur polyscopie, leur intersensualité et leur caractère poétique.

Epilogue: Culture de fusion

Bollywood est aujourd'hui bien plus qu'une industrie cinématographique. C'est une industrie culturelle globale qui comprend outre le film, la danse et la musique, également la mode et le textile, l'économie touristique, les accessoires et les produits cosmétiques, le mobilier et la décoration, les produits nutritifs et la cuisine, ainsi que le business internet et même la littérature. Le succès du roman de Shashi Tharoor «Bollywood» ou de l'essai monumental de Suketu Mehta, que je cite ici abondamment, «Bombay, Maximum City», peuvent être vu de cette perspective.

Ce succès de Bollywood est à l'Ouest, lui, plus équivoque. Il reste en effet moins l'indice d'un intérêt pour l'Inde et les différents cinémas indiens qu'une nostalgie inassouvie pour de nouveaux mondes d'images fortes: une sorte de voyage refoulant ou ignorant les différences de perception, de sensibilité et les différences culturelles considérables.

---

39 Paul Rabinow: Repräsentationen sind soziale Tatsachen. In: Eberhard Berg / Martin Fuchs (ed.): Kultur, soziale Praxis, Text. Die Krise der ethnographischen repräsentation, Suhrkamp, Francfort 1993, p. 158-199.

Le problème du terme orientalisme, c'est qu'il reste trop lié au travail de d'Edward Said. Il récupère donc les lacunes de l'essai célèbre de l'auteur[40], en particulier celle bien connue de la dichotomie entre Orient et Occident, qui n'est pas mise en question. Said, on le sait, esquisse une interprétation idéaliste des relations entre Orient et Occident qui n'aide non seulement pas à dissoudre cette dichotomie construite entre est et Ouest mais la fixe et la rigidifie.[41]

Il convient également de prendre ses distances avec les formes de néo-orientalisme qui réhabilitent certaines thèses culturalistes de l'orientalisme classique dans un contexte d'idéologisation des relations des pays d'Asie du Sud-Est ou des pays musulmans avec les pays dits occidentaux, favorisant par là une lecture essentialiste du champ religieux hindouiste, islamique, sikhs, etc. On les reconnaît souvent à leur manière de prendre ces champs culturels et religieux comme des unités cohérentes et statiques et de considérer, même de manière non-formulée, la modernité comme fondamentalement occidentale dans son contenu et ses formes. C'est une des erreurs que le Bollywood de Gowariker, Karan Johan ou Farah Khan surmonte allègrement, sans avoir à nier les différences qui le caractérisent.

Il existe des régimes du regard dans les cinémas indiens, dans les scènes de danse par exemple, qui ne connaissent pas d'équivalent occidental comme celui, sensuel, appelé Nazar qui renvoie à la poésie perse ou encore celui nommé «drishti» qui renvoie à la tradition religieuse hindoue.[42] Il existe de la même manière des régimes du regard sur l'apparence qui joue avec les tissus, les couleurs et les formes et vont aussi bien dans le sens d'un enfermement du corps que dans celui de sa découverte. La dénudation crue du corps et le jeu minimaliste du textile qu'offre les pays de l'ouest n'est là qu'une option supplémentaire mais certainement pas une forme d'émancipation ou une réponse générale aux questions concernant le corps et le gender (genre). En l'adoptant, le cinéma de Bollywood la place sur son propre terrain fantasmatique. Inutile de chercher là un universalisme que le cinéma ne possède heureusement pas.

Pour terminer, je dirai que le vêtement nous suggère une piste pour sortir du dilemme occidentalisme / orientalisme, car la mode est aussi, comme le cinéma, un écran («screen»), c'est-à-dire un interface de projection idéo-logique déterminé, structuré justement par le régime du regard. Il existe cependant des

---

40 Edward Said: Orientalism. Penguin Books, London 1995 (1979). Voir aussi dans le même ordre mais concentré sur l'Inde Ronald Inden: Imagining India. Blackwell, Oxford/GB et Cambridge/USA 1990. Tous deux s'appuient essentiellement sur des sources littéraires pour étayer leurs thèses.
41 Voir à ce sujet Sadia Jalal al-Azm: Orientalism and Orientalism in Reverse. Alexandre Lyon Macfie (ed.), Orientalism. A Reader. New York 2000, p. 217-238.
42 De l'arabe nazar pour regard, le mot renvoie à la tradition poétique perse. Woodman Tylor: Visual Display in Popular Indian Cinema. Sumathi Ramaswamy (dir.), Beyond Apparences? Visual Practices and Ideologies in Modern India, New Delhi, London 2003, p. 301-306. Un autre est drishti, un régime du regard qui renvoie lui à la tradition religieuse indoue.

ruptures dans le champ du visuel, du visible (Jacques Lacan) – dont le vêtement fait partie intégrante, dynamique -, des ruptures qui irritent, sont instables et mouvantes ou même insoumises et dans lesquels s'engouffrent d'autres mondes de significations.

J'opterai donc ici pour ces ruptures, pour la perspective du *beyond* et le concept de culture de fusion. Un tel concept me semble tout à fait adéquat pour travailler la complexité des échanges interculturels urbains aujourd'hui.

Ce terme de fusion provient des réflexions et pratiques des milieux multiculturels dans les grandes métropoles comme New York, Londres, la banlieue Parisienne ou Mumbay. Il offre déjà au niveau vestimentaire une possibilité de négociation à la fois *avec* et *au-delà* des réservoirs d'images que sont devenues aujourd'hui l'orientalisme et l'occidentalisme.

C'est la misère et la richesse dialectiques de cette époque, résolument liées à la modernité globale, que de pouvoir mêler des éléments auparavant inconciliables. Images de soi, images de l'autre et jeux de miroirs s'y croisent, s'interpénêtent et se renvoient y opérant un effet fusionnel. Les acteurs sociaux y utilisent – et ce faisant les redécouvrent – des techniques corporelles et des pratiques sociales liées à leur(s) culture(s) locale(s) d'origine en rapports avec leurs biographies individuelles mais pour mieux jouer avec elles et les détourner, parfois même radicalement.

Ciment de l'imaginaire culturel des Non Residents Indians à travers le monde, Bollywood est devenu aussi un bagage du jeune public occidental. Il peut alors bien y devenir un lieu vestimentaire de transit, non obligatoire[43], et bien sûr une porte d'accès à la large culture cinématographique et vestimentaire de l'Inde et par là-même à ses richesses fusionnelles, anciennes et nouvelles.

Films cités

3 Idiots (2009) de Raijkumar Hirani
Amrapali (1966) de Lekh Tandon
Autant en emporte le vent (1939) de Victor Fleming
Bandit Queen (1994) de Shekar Kappur
Black (2005) de Sanjay Leela Bhansali
Chantons sous la pluie (1952) de Stanley Donen et Gene Kelly
Cléopâtre (1963). Josef Mankiewicz
Devdas (2002) de Sanjay Leela Bhansali
Dilwale Dulhania le Jayenge (1995) de Aditya Chopra
Don 2. The King is back (2011) de Farhan Akhtar
Fire (1996) de Deepa Mehta
Ghajini (2008) de A.R. Murugadoss

---

43 Pour les Non Residents Indians Bollywood n'est pas seulement une distraction mais prend la valeur d'un espace imaginaire culturel quasi existentiel, une sorte de lien émotionnel avec leur culture qui les unit en une véritable communauté.

Jodhaa Akbar (2008) de Ashutosh Gowariker
Humjoli (1970) de Ramanna
Jay – Vejay 2 (1977) de L.V. Prasad
Kabhi Alvida Naa Kehna (2006) de Karan Johar
Kal Hoo Naa Ho (2003) de Nikhil Advani
Karz (1980) de Subhash Gai
Lagaan. Once upon in India (2001) de Ashutosh Gowariker
Kuch Kuch Hota Hai 81998) de Karan Johar
Main Hoon Na (2004) de Farah Khan
Maqbool (2003) de Vishal Bhardwaj
Monsoom Wedding (2001) de Mira Nair
My Name is Khan (2009) de Karan Johar
Om Shanti Om (2007) de Farah Khan
Paheli (2005) de Amol Palekar
Suzie et les Backers Boys (1989) de Steven Kloves
Swades (2004) de Ashutosh Gowariker
Umrao Jaan (2006) de Jyoti Prakash Dutta.

Glossaire

Choli: Veste/chemisier très court à manches longues ou trois-quart laissant voir le ventre. Porté avec le sari ou le lehanga.
Churidar: Pantalon large dans le style du shalwar porté par les hommes et les femmes. Porté généralement avec une tunique.
Dhoti: Vêtement traditionnel indien des hommes, pièce de tissu passée entre les jambes et nouée autour de la taille ou portée en forme de pantalon. L'art de l'agencer change d'une region à l'autre et prend des formes et des tailles très variées
Duppata: Pièce de tissues en forme de large écharpe portée avec le sari.
Fargi: Manteau d'apparat à manches trois-quart.
Gaghra: Jupe longue décorée.
Ghatchola: Large et somptueuse écharpe porté sur une epaule ou drapée autour du torse. Portée généralement sur un sari ou un lehanga.
Haveli: Demeure aisée ou petit palais.
Jamavar: Châle somptueux.
Kantha: Echarpe richement décorée.
Kotha: Maison close, maison de plaisir.
Ksatriyas: Une des quatre Varna ("Castes") du modèle hindou hégémonique brahmane. Un des type de "castes" d'option guerrière le plus cité dans l'histoire du monde indien.
Kurta: Chemise ample descendant jusqu'aux genoux.
Lehanga: Longue jupe légèrement traînante de sortie ou d'apparat, portée souvent avec un choli ou/et un châle. Très en mode. Connaît de nombreuses variations.

Lungi: Pièce de tissue rectangulaire d'homme enroulée autour de la taille.
Odhani: Long voile généralement brodé de fil de soie, tombant dans le dos.
Peshwas: Longue robe très ceintrée et s'élargissant fortement à partir de la taille. Portée originairement par les hommes et les femmes, la mode d'aujourd'hui a créé des formes variées de peshwas féminines.
Pyjama: Large pantaloon.
Radha: Troisième figure de la mythologie krishnienne (évoquée par exemple dans les Puranas et surtout le Mahabharata, l'épopée sanskrite de la mythologie hindoue), Radha est la compagne et l'amante éternelle de Krishna ("Jamais ensemble mais toujours unis" dit un dialogue de *Lagaan*).
Salwar kameez: Originairement tenue des femmes musulmanes, le salwar kameez s'est élargi à toute la société indienne, comme mode feminine très pratique, surtout chez les jeunes generations. Connaît entretemps des formes très modernes (par exemple avec des tuniques plus courtes).
Sari: Vêtement traditionnel des femmes hindoues. Originairement d'orientation religieuse, le sari, s'est lui aussi propagé comme mode, bien qu'avec moins de succes que le shalwar kameez, dans toute la société indienne. Composé d'une longue pièce rectangulaire drapant plusiuers fois la taille et les jambes, ainsi que d'un choli et d'une duppatta sur les épaules, le sari connaît de très nombreuses variations dans la manière de l'agencer.
Sherwani: Longue tenue d'apparat en forme de manteau à petit col et richement décorée.

Fig. 1 : *Devdas*. Chandramukhi (Madhuri Dixit)

Fig. 2. *Lagaan* : Kachra (Aditya Lakhia)

Fig. 3 : *Kal Ho Naa Ho* : Amman (Shah Rukh Khan), Naina (Preity Zinta) et le KHNH-Bridge.

Fig. 4 : *Kuch Kuch Hota Hai.* Anjeli (Kajol) et Rahul (ShahRukh Khan)

Fig. 5 : *Om Shanti Om* : Shantipriya (Deepika Padukone) et Om (Shah Rukh Khan)

Summaries

Buyun Chen, Dept. of East Asian Languages and Cultures of Columbia University, New York
„Toward a Definition of "Fashion" in Tang Dynasty China (618-907CE)"

By the mid-eighth century, the women of the reigning emperor's court had abandoned the slim silhouettes of their predecessors and opted for broader sleeves and expansive skirts. These voluptuous figures, cloaked in heavily embroidered silk gauzes and framed by lofty piles of hair, articulated an emergent self-fashioning impulse that hinted at a new order of appearances.

Over the course of the dynasty, styles of dress and adornment expanded to incorporate new silhouettes and patterns to satisfy the Tang woman's impulse to make and re-make the self. Fashion's rise in the Tang dynasty signaled a process, in which status competition and self-identification among the elites gradually broke away from the imperial court and official ranks, thereby transforming the dressed body into a stage for status display. By the late ninth century, changes in the economic and political structure gave rise to a new fashionable elite whose politics of appearance was now dictated by an aspiration to be "timely" or "in time." In this paper, fashion is not defined as the rapid transformation of styles governed by high overturn of fabrics that serve as passing signifiers of commodity fetishism, but is understood as a system of social practices manufactured by material relations and embroiled in the politics of self and body. In a shift away from the "fashion" *is* "change" construction that is rooted in industrial capitalism and Western modernity, this paper provides ways of thinking about fashion in its root sense as a process of making.

Gabriele Mentges, Technische Universität Dortmund, Germany.
"Drawing Borders: Perceptions of the Cultural Other in Renaissance Costume Books"

The essay examines the significance of Renaissance costume books and their role in paving the way for orientalist discourses and practices. The scholarly significance of clothing and fashion in descriptions of the Other is particularly important. An analysis of different themes and transformations of the motifs in the images demonstrates that the books contain an aesthetic hierarchy and moral evaluations; these were used not only to give shape to and strengthen the European identity but also increasingly excluded the cultural Other—Arabs, Indians, Africans, and Asians—on grounds of moral inferiority. Fashion/clothing is, in this context, an important category and factor in the establishment of an aesthetic hegemony of the West.

Gertrud Lehnert, Universität Potsdam, Germany
"Orientalism in 18th and 19th Century Fashion Magazines"

18th and 19th century fashion magazines (like the „Cabinet des Modes" or the „Moniteur de la Mode") seem to be perfect illustrations of Edward Said's analysis of the Orient as a construction of the West, aimed at forging the West's proper identity via the oriental other. However, Said's theory has to be differentiated and enlarged in order to properly analyze fashion in terms of material culture and fantasy production.

My chapter has two arguments. First, I focus on the construction of two key concepts of both fashion and of Orientalism in the magazines: imitation seems obvious; less obvious is performativity – an early example of an analytical category current en vogue in cultural studies. Secondly, I discuss the ways early magazines use texts and images in order not only to describe fashion, but to suggest certain emotions and atmospheres of orientalizing Western fashion. What effects do each of the two media generate? How is the combination of media realized: as a simple addition of two media? Or as iconotextuality? How do they convey the fantasies and atmospheres indispensable for „fashion"?

Mona Abaza, The American University in Cairo, Egypt
"The Motahajiba in Cairo, Inter - Arab Islamic Chic, Adaptations, Hybridity and Globalization"

This article narrates the success story of the Motahajiba Islamic fashion chains in Egypt as told by its representative in Cairo who opened the first shop in year 2000. The Motahajiba´s main headquarter is based in Qatar. It is owned by the Al-Siddique International Group, which was created in 1981. The Motahajiba has established 23 branches in the GCC (the Gulf countries) and in Egypt. They claim to be the first and only factory in Qatar known to produce the 'Abaya, Shela (Sheila) and Hijab (head cover). By analyzing the narrative of the local Egyptian branch of such an international (inter-Arab, inter-Islamic) fashion chain, I draw attention to the inventions and adaptations of the "khaliji" taste 1 catering to Egyptian customers. This is undertaken via hybridizing textiles and colours produced in Bombay and Delhi specifically made for the Egyptian upper class customer. Evidently, garments worn in the Gulf countries would not have been popular in Egypt, had they not undergone significant transformations because of the differing local Arab contexts and the different accessibility of women to public spaces in Egypt in comparison to the Gulf countries.

---

[1] The khalij/khalig (depending on the dialect) is the Arabic word to define the countries from the Gulf, Khaliji is the adjective as well as the proper noun for people of the Gulf.

The Motahajiba chains have been famed for their sophisticated embroidered black scarves exclusively made of black chiffon, which is solely produced in Japan, but embroidered in Doha. From its very start the Motahajiba has been advertised as an upper class and a highly expensive Islamic fashion chain.

The Motahajiba branch in Cairo, on the other hand, drifted slightly apart from the mother company by adapting Moroccan Cafetans, Punjabi outfits, Malay Baju Kurungs and Indonesian styles into the 'proper' Islamic but Egyptianized 'chic' dress. It is important to take into consideration that the khaliji Abaya was seen in Cairene Street only during the past two decades. It is clearly different from the black large sheet the (milayya laff), which was worn by popular, lower class, Cairene women and the peasant female gallabeyyas (long dresses). While previous cosmopolitan-colonial elites identified "good taste" and fashion by emulating European and specifically French taste, language and culture, the post-colonial elites that followed - And in contradistinction to the Indian case for example- hardly ever challenged the introduction and emulation of western apparel in Egypt.

Late President Sadat instigated a state Islamization and encouraged former members of the religious opposition to expand their activities during his reign. He gave further space for religion and religious symbols which grew out of control. However, the phenomenon of the spread of Islamic attire amongst lower classes was perceived as one way of affirming one's identity in particular after the strong feeling of defeat that secularism encouraged in the previous Nasser regime.

The phenomenon of "Islamic chic" is radically different from the anti-consumerist attitudes of the early Islamic opposition, which grew in Egypt the seventies. "Islamic chic" is the result of a massive Islamization of the public sphere leading to multiple readings and usage of Islamic attire. The trend of "Islamic chic" could be understood as an expression of rising consumerist appetites of the new Islamic bourgeoisie much comparable to Turkey. I discuss the issue of Islamic chic within a wider context related to globalization and the rise of new middle classes that underwent the impact of "petro-Islam" and the brand of Islam that was imported from the oil-producing countries.

Pravina Shukla, Indiana University, Bloomington, USA
"The System of Fashion in the East – Dress in Modern India"

The study of Orientalism by Western scholars would be enhanced by an analysis of fashion within the Orient, employing an ethnographic approach to understanding fashion and its place in a coherent cultural system.

Recent scholarship on the topic broadens the orientalist/colonialist view by acknowledging the internal forces at play in the East – global markets and consumer power, production and exchange, gender and class implications. Most of these studies, however, still view the East in relation to the West, a cog in the globalized economic machine of dress and power.

The two cultural forces affecting fashion – the Occidental and the Oriental -- are minor compared to internal forces that guide the conceptualization, creation, exchange, and consumption of items of dress and adornment. By looking at the variety of expression in relation to fashion, from all the participants – designers, makers, merchants, adorned women -- we see that the internal system in the East operates much like the internal system of fashion in the West. The node of cultural exchange happens at the local level, where external influences, for example from the West or Bollywood, are internalized, modified for local appropriation and consumption.

The next move is to gather the majority of the players who do not wear Western fashion, do not interact or react with the Western globalized markets, but who do affect the internal system of dress.

Employing an ethnographic approach to the study of contemporary fashion and its place in a coherent cultural system within India, I draw on my extensive fieldwork in the northeast of India.

Yuniya (Yuni) Kawamura, Fashion Institute of Technology New York, USA
"The Globalization of Japanese Lolita Fashion".

There are different types of fashion and subcultures in Harajuku, one of the most fashionable districts in Tokyo. A Lolita look, which is the exaggerated form of femininity and which looks like a Victorian doll, is the most popular style among the teens who congregate near the Harajuku station on weekends. This particular fashion subculture has spread globally and is found in the U.S. as well as Europe. In my chapter, I explore who they are, how they dress, what it means to be part of the Lolita community, and what this phenomenon means to the society. It is meant to be exemplary for the analysis of youth cultures in fashion and the way they use old and new, oriental and occidental elements in order to create their own "fusion" style between cultures and ages.

Oly Firsching-Tovar, Technische Universität Dortmund, Germany
"Reviving Kimono: Fashion as Memory at the Turn of the 21st Century"

This chapter is based on the analysis of documents and of photos collected while doing ethnographic fieldwork during the fall of 2008 in Kyoto, Japan.

Newly published pocket-sized books on the themes of kimono, kimono design and local tourism that were found at second hand kimono boutiques, museums or at book shops, have been printed and published in Japan (since year 2000) and target exclusively young natives, mostly girls interested in contemporary kimono culture.

Through the analysis of a chapter in one of the pocket-sized books, named „Kimono at Kyoto", the paper examines how local kimono designers and consumers seem to be attracted to a specific period of Japanese modern history, known as „Taishō Roman".

The chapter tries to summarize the process by which kimonos of the period (1912-1926) were influenced by the Japanese artistic and literary movement known as „Taishō Romanticism". It analyzes how this style of kimono known as „Taishō Roman" has been revived and how and why some characteristics of the look of the women of those years of Japanese history, inspire kimono fashion designers, coordinators and consumers today.

The fusion and mixture of Japanese and Western styles of art and design blossoming during the Taishō period, also called „Taishō Chic", happened at a time when Western fashion and its consuming practices were assimilated in Japan. The chapter explores how a kind of „Memory Culture" of this period of Japanese history has been used and updated, making the kimono fashionable and marketable for young Japanese consumers today.

Daniel Devoucoux, Technische Universität Dortmund, Germany.
"Orientalism plus Occidentalism or the costume politics of the "New Bollywood movies" (since the 90ties onward)

The striking success of Bollywood movies in the West since the 1990s seems to revoke at first sight a return of Orientalism, because neither film critics nor the press in general take into account the differences of their imagery of space and time, of the sensual experiences and the ways of perception.

Therefore the article discusses two main aspects: How is the reception of Bollywood movies by the Western audience constructed? and how are the new Bollywood films organized?

Meanwhile the new Bollywood films pursue double goals: a successful marketing strategy inside as well as outside India. Thus, the paper intends to analyse which imagery of Orientalism/Occidentalism regarding fashion is negotiated, because fashion practices seem to be the best means to articulate the different ways of perception, sensibility and attitudes. Moreover, the article draws attention to the fact that, at the same time, "Orientalism" refers to a term of crisis.

The play with fashion and pictures and the process of transfer and appropriation associated with them are ambivalent and move in both directions. They can no longer be interpreted on the basis of the post-colonial theory of the cinema. Indian stories filmed in New York or London don´t necessarily deal with American or English cultures. Instead, what becomes particularly relevant is the way they speak about themselves in the context of these cities. Also, the reasons for the fascination of the Western public of Bollywood movies differ from the pleasure of the Indian spectator in particular in regard to sartorial questions. The global circulation of the cinematic gaze is not equivalent with open exchange, instead it furthers the maintenance of local meanings with new methods and new looks.

Authors

Mona Abaza
Professor of Sociology in the Department of Sociology, Anthropology, Psychology and Egytology at the American University in Cairo, Egypt
Her publications include:
* Twentieth Century Egyptian Art: The Private Collection of Sherwet Shafei, The American University Press 2011
* The Changing Consumer Culture of Modern Egypt. Cairo's Urban Reshaping, Brill/AUC Press 2006
* Debates on Islam and Knowledge in Malaysia and Egypt: Shifting Worlds, Routledge Curzon Press 2002

Bu Yun Chen
PhD Student at the Dept. of East Asian Languages and Cultures of Columbia University, New York
She is currently completing her dissertation research in Beijing, China. Her dissertation investigates the emergence of fashion in the Tang Dynasty (618 - 907) through an integrated approach of history and material culture studies.

Daniel Devoucoux
Teacher at the department Art and Material Culture TU-Dortmund, Teaching and research focus on media and fashion, fashion history,
His publications include
*Fashion World – World Fashion. In: Progress Europe. Culture report, Stuttgart 2007, S. 263-275.
*Mode im Film. Zur Kulturanthropologie zweier Medien. Berlin 2007.
*Die Kunst des Andeutens. Die Dinge und ihr Double im Film und Fernsehen. Gudrun König / Gabriele Mentges (ed.): Medien der Mode, Berlin Ebersbach 2010, p. 76-97.
*Elizabeth 1ère de Shehar Kapur ou le rôle du costume au cinéma. Isabelle Paresys / Natacha Coquery (ed.) : Se vêtir à la cour en Europe 1400-1815, Paris2011, S. 257-277.

Oly Firsching-Tovar
Master of Fine Arts, University of Arts Kanazawa , Japan, several awards by the Ministry of Education und Culture, Japan.
Since 2009 PdH Student at the department of Art and Material Culture, TU Dortmund
She is currently completing her dissertation research on the recycling of kimono in Japanese society of today (ethnographic field research in Japan)

Yuniya Kawamura
Assistant Professor of Sociology at the Fashion Institute of Technology New York, USA. She completed her Ph.D. dissertation at Columbia University, and is also professionally trained as a fashion designer and a patternmaker at Bunka School of Fashion in Japan, Kingston Polytechnic in England, and FIT.
Her publications include:
* Fashioning Japanese Subcultures, London: Bloomsbury Academic 2012
* Fashion-ology, An Introduction to Fashion Studies, Oxford, New York 2005
* The Japanese Revolution in Paris Fashion, Oxford, New York: Berg Publishers 2004

Gertrud Lehnert
Professor of Comparative Literature and Cultural Studies at the University of Potsdam. Her research focusses on the theory and history of fashion. She is the editor of a Series „Fashion Studies", Transcript Verlag, Bielefeld
Her publications include:
* Mode. Ein Schnellkurs, Köln: Dumont Buchverlag 1998 (4. edition 2008; translated into English, Japanese, Chinese, Korean, Hungarian, Swedish, Norwegian etc.)
* Frauen machen Mode. Modeschöpferinnen vom 18. Jahrhundert bis heute. Dortmund: edition ebersbach 1998 (wieder München: Piper Verlag 2000)
* Die Kunst der Mode, Oldenburg: dbv 2006 (ed.)
*Räume der Mode, München: Wilhelm Fink Verlag 2012 (ed.)
*Forthcoming: Mode. Theorie, Geschichte und Ästhetik einer kulturellen Praxis, 2014

Gabriele Mentges
Professor of Cultural Anthropology of Material Culture at the department Art and Material Culture, TU Dortmund, research and teaching focus on fashion history, museology, design history, body and gender history, Co-editor of Dortmunder Studien zur Kulturanthropologie des Textilen (6 volumes)
Her publications include:
*Mentges, G. / Richard, Birgit (Hg.): Die Schönheit der Uniformität. Campus, Frankfurt am Main und New York 2005.
*Mentges, Gabriele (Hg.): Kulturanthropologie des Textilen. Berlin, Dortmund 2005.
*Mentges, Gabriele, Neuland, Dagmar, Richard, Birgit (Hrsg.): Uniformierung in Bewegung. Vestimentäre Praktiken zwischen Vereinheitlichung, Kostümierung und Maskerade. Waxmann, Münster, New York 2007
König,G./Gabriele Mentges. (Hg.): Medien der Mode. Dortmunder Studien zur Kulturanthropologie des Textilen, 6. Berlin 2010
*Forthcoming: Gabriele Mentges/Lola Shamukhitdinova (ed.): Modernity of Traditions Uzbek Textile Heritage as Cultural and Economic Resource. Münster/New York 2013

Pravina Shukla
Associate Professor at the Department of Folklore and Ethnomusicology at Indiana University, Bloomington, USA
Her publications include:
* The Grace of Four Moons: Dress, Adornment, and the Art of the Body in Modern India, Bloomington: Indiana University Press, 2008
* "Dress, Costume, and Bodily Adornment as Material Culture," Special Issue, Midwestern Folklore, 32(1/2) (spring/fall 2006). (ed.).
* The Individual and Tradition: Folkloristic Perspectives (Bloomington: Indiana University Press, 2011 (co-Ed.)

List of illustrations

Toward a definition of "fashion" in Tang China (BuYun Chan)
Figure 1: Quianling Museum, Shaanxi Province
Figure 2: Shaanxi History Museum, Xi´an.

Drawing Borders: Perceptions of Cultural Other in Renaissance Costume Books (Gabriele Mentges)
Figure 1: Christoph Weiditz: Trachtenbuch. Courtesy Germanisches Nationalmuseum Nuremberg, Germany. Hs 22474, Picture 203.
Figure 2: Sigmundt Heldt: Abconterfaitting allerley Ordenspersonen. Courtesy Staatliche Museen zu Berlin, Lipperheidesche Kostümbibliothek Berlin, Lipp Aa 3, S. 362.
Figure 3: Abraham de Bruyn. Omnie poene gentium imagines. Courtesy Staatliche Museen zu Berlin, Lipperheidesche Kostümbibliothek Berlin. Lipp Aa 15. „Also gehen die Moriskofrauen".
Figure 4: Jean-Jacques Boissard. Habitus variarum orbis gentium. 1581. Courtesy Staatliche Museen zu Berlin, Lipperheidesche Kostümbibliothek Berlin. Lipp Aa 22, S. 61. Femina India Orientalis.

Orientalism in 18. and 19. Century Fashion Magazines (Gertrud Lehnert)
Figure 1: Cabinet des modes, 15 january 1786: Femme en robe à la Turque. Courtesy Staatliche Museen zu Berlin, Kunstbibliothek, Sammlung Modebild – Lipperheidesche Kostümbibliothek.
Figure 2: *Journal des Dames et des Modes, 1847, Tome 98, vol. 2, p 255*. Courtesy Staatliche Museen zu Berlin, Kunstbibliothek, Sammlung Modebild – Lipperheidesche Kostümbibliothek.
Figure 3: *Moniteur de la Mode 1880, 28. Februar, gravure 1687*. Courtesy Staatliche Museen zu Berlin, Kunstbibliothek, Sammlung Modebild – Lipperheidesche Kostümbibliothek)
Figure 4: *Cabinet des Modes, 31. cahier, 20.9.1788, planche II et III, p. 246: Robe à l'angloise and „Negligé du serrail"*. Courtesy Staatliche Museen zu Berlin, Kunstbibliothek, Sammlung Modebild – Lipperheidesche Kostümbibliothek.

The Motahajiba in Cairo, Inter-Arab Islamic Chic, Adaptations, Hybridity and Globalization (Mona Abaza)
Pictures by Mona Abaza.

The System of Fashion in the East: The Sari in Modern India (Pravina Shukla)
Figure 1: Extra weft silk Banarasi sari in the *jangli mina* design. Banaras, Uttar Pradesh, 2001. Photo by Pravina Shukla.
Figure 2: Sari weaver Hashim Ansari at his family atelier, Sonarpura neighborhood, Banaras, Uttar Pradesh, 2003. Photo by Henry Glassie.
Figure 3: Sari shop in Dashaswamedh Road commercial center, Banaras, Uttar Pradesh, 2003. Photo by Pravina Shukla.
Figure 4: Nina Khanchandani outside of her home. Banaras, Uttar Pradesh, 2003. Photo by Henry Glassie.
Figure 5: Mukta Tripathi, outside of her home, Banaras, Uttar Pradesh, 2003. Photo by Henry Glassie.

The Globalization of Japanese Lolita Fashion (Yuniya Kawamura)
Figure 1: Punk Lolita in Tokyo: Model-Sara; Photo-Courtesy of Kera Magazine

Figure 2: Classic Lolita in Tokyo: Model-Manami Abe; Photo by Masato Imai.
Figure 3: Sweet Lolitas in Paris; Photo-Courtesy of Tenkai-Japan.
Figure 4: Sweet Lolita in New York; Photo by Yuniya Kawamura
Figure 5: Sweet Lolita in New York; Photo by Yuniya Kawamura
Figure 6: Elegant Gothic Lolita in Treviso, Italy: Model-Silvia Nodari

Reviving Kimono: Fashion as Memory at the Turn of the Twenty-First Century (Oly Firsching-Tovar)
Figure 1. Taken from the frontspiece of the mook "Kimono At Kyoto". Edited and printed in Japan in year 2005 by Mitsumura Suiko Shoin.
Figure 2. Photo by Oly Firsching-Tovar. Kyoto October 2008.

Bollywood ou la réinvention de l'orientalisme et de l'occidentalisme dans le cinéma indien actuel (Daniel Devoucoux)
Figure 1 : Cinema. Devdas. http://www.cinema.de/bilder/devdas-flamme-unserer-liebe,1305660.html
Figure 2 : From Lagaan. Once Upon A Time in India. Columbia TriStar Film.
Figure 3 : TV-Spielfilm. Kal Ho Naa Ho. Indian Love Story
Figure 4 : TV-Spielfilm. Kuch Kuch Hota hai.
http://www.funonline.in/wp-content/uploads/2012/01/Kajol-in-Kuch-Kuch-Hota-Hai.jpg
Figure 5 : Movie Outnow. Om Shanti Om.
http://outnow.ch/Movies/2007/OmShantiOm/Bilder/movie.ws/01

www.ingramcontent.com/pod-product-compliance
Ingram Content Group UK Ltd.
Pitfield, Milton Keynes, MK11 3LW, UK
UKHW021904240426
12048UKWH00045B/647